A3 Status Report

Author: _____

Date: _____

Theme:

Background:

Target Statement:

Implementation Status:

Action	Responsibility	Due	Complete

Impact:

Unresolved Issues:

A3 Status Report

Author: _____

Date: _____

Theme:

Background:

Impact:

Target Statement:

Implementation Status:

Action	Responsibility	Due	Complete

Unresolved Issues:

www.enna.com

A3 Status Report

Author: _____

Date: _____

Theme:

Background:

Target Statement:

Implementation Status:

Action	Responsibility	Due	Complete

Impact:

Unresolved Issues:

www.enna.com

A3 Status Report

Author: _____

Date: _____

Theme:

Background:

Target Statement:

Impact:

Implementation Status:

Action	Responsibility	Due	Complete

Unresolved Issues:

A3 Status Report

Author: _____

Date: _____

Theme:

Background:

Target Statement:

Implementation Status:

Action	Responsibility	Due	Complete

Impact:

Unresolved Issues:

A3 Status Report

Author: _____

Date: _____

Theme:

Background:

Impact:

Target Statement:

Implementation Status:

Action	Responsibility	Due	Complete

Unresolved Issues:

www.enna.com

A3 Status Report

Author: _____

Date: _____

Theme:

Background:

Target Statement:

Impact:

Implementation Status:

Action	Responsibility	Due	Complete

Unresolved Issues:

A3 Status Report

Author: _____

Date: _____

Theme:

Background:

Impact:

Target Statement:

Implementation Status:

Action	Responsibility	Due	Complete

Unresolved Issues:

www.enna.com

A3 Status Report

Author: _____

Date: _____

Theme:

Background:

Impact:

Target Statement:

Implementation Status:

Action	Responsibility	Due	Complete

Unresolved Issues:

A3 Status Report

Author: _____

Date: _____

Theme:

Background:

Impact:

Target Statement:

Implementation Status:

Action	Responsibility	Due	Complete

Unresolved Issues:

© ENNA
KNOWLEDGE INTO PRACTICE

www.enna.com

A3 Status Report

Author: _____

Date: _____

Theme:

Background:

Impact:

Target Statement:

Implementation Status:

Action	Responsibility	Due	Complete

Unresolved Issues:

www.enna.com

A3 Status Report

Author: _____

Date: _____

Theme:

Background:

Target Statement:

Implementation Status:

Action	Responsibility	Due	Complete

Impact:

Unresolved Issues:

© ENNA
KNOWLEDGE INTO PRACTICE

www.enna.com

A3 Status Report

Author: _____

Date: _____

Theme:

Background:

Impact:

Target Statement:

Implementation Status:

Action	Responsibility	Due	Complete

Unresolved Issues:

A3 Status Report

Author: _____

Date: _____

Theme:

Background:

Target Statement:

Impact:

Unresolved Issues:

Implementation Status:

Action	Responsibility	Due	Complete

www.enna.com

A3 Status Report

Author: _____

Date: _____

Theme:

Background:

Impact:

Target Statement:

Implementation Status:

Action	Responsibility	Due	Complete

Unresolved Issues:

A3 Status Report

Author: _____

Date: _____

Theme:

Background:

Target Statement:

Implementation Status:

Action	Responsibility	Due	Complete

Impact:

Unresolved Issues:

A3 Status Report

Author: _____

Date: _____

Theme:

Background:

Target Statement:

Impact:

Implementation Status:

Action	Responsibility	Due	Complete

Unresolved Issues:

A3 Status Report

Author: _____

Date: _____

Theme:

Background:

Target Statement:

Implementation Status:

Action	Responsibility	Due	Complete

Impact:

Unresolved Issues:

www.enna.com

A3 Status Report

Author: _____

Date: _____

Theme:

Background:

Impact:

Target Statement:

Implementation Status:

Action	Responsibility	Due	Complete

Unresolved Issues:

A3 Status Report

Author: _____

Date: _____

Theme:

Background:

Target Statement:

Implementation Status:

Action	Responsibility	Due	Complete

Impact:

Unresolved Issues:

www.enna.com

A3 Status Report

Author: _____

Date: _____

Theme:

Background:

Target Statement:

Implementation Status:

Action	Responsibility	Due	Complete

Impact:

Unresolved Issues:

A3 Status Report

Author: _____

Date: _____

Theme:

Background:

Impact:

Target Statement:

Implementation Status:

Action	Responsibility	Due	Complete

Unresolved Issues:

A3 Status Report

Author: _____

Date: _____

Theme:

Background:

Target Statement:

Implementation Status:

Action	Responsibility	Due	Complete

Impact:

Unresolved Issues:

A3 Status Report

Author: _____

Date: _____

Theme:

Background:

Target Statement:

Implementation Status:

Action	Responsibility	Due	Complete

Impact:

Unresolved Issues:

5S Evaluation Review

T0156168

Date: _____   Evaluation Area: _____

5S Element	Number	Evaluation Criteria	Rank these items from 1 through 5: 5 being well done	Score (1-5)	Ideas / Suggestions / Comments
SORT	I	Are the aisles and walkways open and clear?	All items that are not necessary or unsafe have been removed from the area where people travel and work.		
	II	Is the work zone free of any spills of fluids?	Consider whether there are any chemicals, lubricants, water, oils or other materials that may be hazardous in the area and on the floor.		
	III	Is the work zone free of unnecessary articles and items?	Are items that are not needed been removed from the work zone, i.e. tools, jigs, stationary, extra items.		
	IV	Is the work zone free of excess consumables/materials?	Evaluate against how many items are in the production work zone. Assess if the materials, parts, and supplies are currently needed for operations.		
	V	Is the information board active?	All announcements are displayed currently and in good presentable shape. Arrangement is straight and placed under appropriate headings.		
	VI	Are the areas walls and dividers free of items not used in operations?	Extra items are not on the walls, dividers, or hanging of signs that are not necessary.		
		Category Subtotal		- - - - -	
		Sort Score: Subtotal divided by 6			
SET IN ORDER / STRAIGHTEN	VII	Evaluate any documentation storage.	Only documents to do the job are stored at the work zone. These documents are stored nicely and in an orderly fashion that is recognizable to outsiders.		
	VIII	How are the shelves, desks, and work surfaces arranged?	All locations of items are labeled, marked, and it is known if they are missing.		
	IX	How are the tools and material used in operations stored?	No items are resting on walls or tucked in corners. No items are resting on equipment, cupboards, or other fixtures.		
	X	Evaluate container and packaging locations and tidiness.	Materials, boxes, storage containers, and other items are stored in the appropriate place and orientated well for operations. Also, they are secure and not causing any danger to the workforce.		
	XI	Assess order and where items are found on the floor.	Nothing is sitting directly on the floor and no materials are left around the area. Items that need to be on the floor are clearly marked and positioned in designated areas clearly outlined on the floor.		
	XII	Easiness to access the tools for machines and measuring gauges.	Materials, tools, jigs, attachments, and fixtures are organized so that they are all easily within reach of the operator. Consider this as well for any kind of measuring tool or go/no-go devices.		
		Category Subtotal		- - - - -	
		Set in Order / Straighten Score: Subtotal divided by 6			
SHINE / SWEEP	XIII	The storage of gauges and tooling.	Arrangement of all fixtures, tools, and attachments are kept in clean area for storage and no risk of damage during transporting to storage.		
	XIV	Clear when equipment needs maintenance and when last maintained.	Buttons and switches on machinery marked, highlighted, and labeled. Check sheets clean and displayed. Maintenance is scheduled; levels of fluids, lubrication of joints are clearly itemized and illustrated.		
	XV	Assess the cleanliness of the work zone.	How dust free are the areas. Look under desks and behind work spaces to see if there is garbage and other unnecessary items.		
	XVI	Safety of the equipment, are areas gated off and safe for workers?	Spray shields and physical guards are in active use to keep items and liquids getting on the floor. Areas that are critical are clearly marked to protect workers.		
	XVII	Assess status of equipment in the area. Cleanliness overall appearance.	Are machines and equipment known to be on a schedule of cleaning?		
		Category Subtotal		- - - - -	
		Shine / Sweep Score: Subtotal divided by 5			
STANDARDIZE	XVIII	Is there visual color diagramming and color coding?	A clear and present color coding system is present in the work zone and across the company. It is clear that standards are being maintained and improved on.		
	XIX	Assess the access ways in case of emergency.	All emergency systems; fire vehicles, fire extinguishers, and emergency equipment free of obstruction and clear at all times. Access to electrical controls and fuses are known, marked, and free of any obstructions.		
	XX	The aisle ways are bright with light and clearly marked.	Walkways are clearly highlighted for direction, aisle access identified at any moment while in the work zone.		
	XXI	General area has quantity limits for materials and are marked clearly.	Heights are marked, quantity of materials are known, and min vs. max.		
	XXII	Is there clear document control of information in the work zone?	All information and documentation is controlled, labeled, and revisions are up to date. There are no label-less binders or pieces of paper in the area.		
		Category Subtotal		- - - - -	
		Standardize Score: Subtotal divided by 5			
SUSTAIN	XXIII	The aisle ways are clean and maintenance is clear.	Aisles are never full of anything and are clear for passage. All items and products not stored in the aisle and storage is next to aisle accessible for transportation.		
	XXIV	Illustrations and work zone plans are available to compare against.	5S has a maintenance system that allows for control of change and improvement of 5S in the work zones. Scoring is kept on each of these items and history is present and visible to support future improvement.		
	XXV	Ability for tools to be set back in place of storage.	No self-discipline is necessary to ensure that all tools, dies, jigs, and equipment are put back in the same spot. The effort of putting back should not require organizational skills.		
	XXVI	Evaluate the involvement of supervisors in 5S.	Supervisors are actively involved in the review process of 5S and are supporting improvement activities of the work areas.		
		Category Subtotal		- - - - -	
		Sustain Score: Subtotal divided by 4			**Total "Category Subtotals" divide by 26 average 5S score: TOTAL**

5S Evaluation Review

Date: _____   Evaluation Area: _____

5S Element	Number	Evaluation Criteria	Rank these items from 1 through 5: 5 being well done	Score (1-5)	Ideas / Suggestions / Comments
SORT	I	Are the aisles and walkways open and clear?	All items that are not necessary or unsafe have been removed from the area where people travel and work.		
	II	Is the work zone free of any spills of fluids?	Consider whether there are any chemicals, lubricants, water, oils or other materials that may be hazardous in the area and on the floor.		
	III	Is the work zone free of unnecessary articles and items?	Are items that are not needed been removed from the work zone, i.e. tools, jigs, stationary, extra items.		
	IV	Is the work zone free of excess consumables/materials?	Evaluate against how many items are in the production work zone. Assess if the materials, parts, and supplies are currently needed for operations.		
	V	Is the information board active?	All announcements are displayed currently and in good presentable shape. Arrangement is straight and placed under appropriate headings.		
	VI	Are the areas walls and dividers free of items not used in operations?	Extra items are not on the walls, dividers, or hanging of signs that are not necessary.		
			Category Subtotal		
			Sort Score: Subtotal divided by 6		
SET IN ORDER / STRAIGHTEN	VII	Evaluate any documentation storage.	Only documents to do the job are stored at the work zone. These documents are stored nicely and in an orderly fashion that is recognizable to outsiders.		
	VIII	How are the shelves, desks, and work surfaces arranged?	All locations of items are labeled, marked, and it is known if they are missing.		
	IX	How are the tools and material used in operations stored?	No items are resting on walls or tucked in corners. No items are resting on equipment, cupboards, or other fixtures.		
	X	Evaluate container and packaging locations and tidiness.	Materials, boxes, storage containers, and other items are stored in the appropriate place and orientated well for operations. Also, they are secure and not causing any danger to the workforce.		
	XI	Assess order and where items are found on the floor.	Nothing is sitting directly on the floor and no materials are left around the area. Items that need to be on the floor are clearly marked and positioned in designated areas clearly outlined on the floor.		
	XII	Easiness to access the tools for machines and measuring gauges.	Materials, tools, jigs, attachments, and fixtures are organized so that they are all easily within reach of the operator. Consider this as well for any kind of measuring tool or go/no-go devices.		
			Category Subtotal		
			Set in Order / Straighten Score: Subtotal divided by 6		
SHINE / SWEEP	XIII	The storage of gauges and tooling.	Arrangement of all fixtures, tools, and attachments are kept in clean area for storage and no risk of damage during transporting to storage.		
	XIV	Clear when equipment needs maintenance and when last maintained.	Buttons and switches on machinery marked, highlighted, and labeled. Check sheets clean and displayed. Maintenance is scheduled; levels of fluids, lubrication of joints are clearly itemized and illustrated.		
	XV	Assess the cleanliness of the work zone.	How dust free are the areas. Look under desks and behind work spaces to see if there is garbage and other unnecessary items.		
	XVI	Safety of the equipment, are areas gated off and safe for workers?	Spray shields and physical guards are in active use to keep items and liquids getting on the floor. Areas that are critical are clearly marked to protect workers.		
	XVII	Assess status of equipment in the area. Cleanliness overall appearance.	Are machines and equipment known to be on a schedule of cleaning?		
			Category Subtotal		
			Shine / Sweep Score: Subtotal divided by 5		
STANDARDIZE	XVIII	Is there visual color diagramming and color coding?	A clear and present color coding system is present in the work zone and across the company. It is clear that standards are being maintained and improved on.		
	XIX	Assess the access ways in case of emergency.	All emergency systems; fire vehicles, fire extinguishers, and emergency equipment free of obstruction and clear at all times. Access to electrical controls and fuses are known, marked, and free of any obstructions.		
	XX	The aisle ways are bright with light and clearly marked.	Walkways are clearly highlighted for direction, aisle access identified at any moment while in the work zone.		
	XXI	General area has quantity limits for materials and are marked clearly.	Heights are marked, quantity of materials are known, and min vs. max.		
	XXII	Is there clear document control of information in the work zone?	All information and documentation is controlled, labeled, and revisions are up to date. There are no label-less binders or pieces of paper in the area.		
			Category Subtotal		
			Standardize Score: Subtotal divided by 5		
SUSTAIN	XXIII	The aisle ways are clean and maintenance is clear.	Aisles are never full of anything and are clear for passage. All items and products not stored in the aisle and storage is next to aisle accessible for transportation.		
	XXIV	Illustrations and work zone plans are available to compare against.	5S has a maintenance system that allows for control of change and improvement of 5S in the work zones. Scoring is kept on each of these items and history is present and visible to support future improvement.		
	XXV	Ability for tools to be set back in place of storage.	No self-discipline is necessary to ensure that all tools, dies, jigs, and equipment are put back in the same spot. The effort of putting back should not require organizational skills.		
	XXVI	Evaluate the involvement of supervisors in 5S.	Supervisors are actively involved in the review process of 5S and are supporting improvement activities of the work areas.		
			Category Subtotal		
			Sustain Score: Subtotal divided by 4		

www.enna.com
www.productivitypress.com

Total "Category Subtotals" divide by 26 average 5S score: TOTAL

5S Evaluation Review

Date: _____   Evaluation Area: _____

5S Element	Number	Evaluation Criteria	Rank these items from 1 through 5: 5 being well done	Score (1-5)	Ideas / Suggestions / Comments
SORT	I	Are the aisles and walkways open and clear?	All items that are not necessary or unsafe have been removed from the area where people travel and work.		
	II	Is the work zone free of any spills of fluids?	Consider whether there are any chemicals, lubricants, water, oils or other materials that may be hazardous in the area and on the floor.		
	III	Is the work zone free of unnecessary articles and items?	Are items that are not needed been removed from the work zone, i.e. tools, jigs, stationary, extra items.		
	IV	Is the work zone free of excess consumables/materials?	Evaluate against how many items are in the production work zone. Assess if the materials, parts, and supplies are currently needed for operations.		
	V	Is the information board active?	All announcements are displayed currently and in good presentable shape. Arrangement is straight and placed under appropriate headings.		
	VI	Are the areas walls and dividers free of items not used in operations?	Extra items are not on the walls, dividers, or hanging of signs that are not necessary.		
		Category Subtotal			
		Sort Score: Subtotal divided by 6			
SET IN ORDER / STRAIGHTEN	VII	Evaluate any documentation storage.	Only documents to do the job are stored at the work zone. These documents are stored nicely and in an orderly fashion that is recognizable to outsiders.		
	VIII	How are the shelves, desks, and work surfaces arranged?	All locations of items are labeled, marked, and it is known if they are missing.		
	IX	How are the tools and material used in operations stored?	No items are resting on walls or tucked in corners. No items are resting on equipment, cupboards, or other fixtures.		
	X	Evaluate container and packaging locations and tidiness.	Materials, boxes, storage containers, and other items are stored in the appropriate place and orientated well for operations. Also, they are secure and not causing any danger to the workforce.		
	XI	Assess order and where items are found on the floor.	Nothing is sitting directly on the floor and no materials are left around the area. Items that need to be on the floor are clearly marked and positioned in designated areas clearly outlined on the floor.		
	XII	Easiness to access the tools for machines and measuring gauges.	Materials, tools, jigs, attachments, and fixtures are organized so that they are all easily within reach of the operator. Consider this as well for any kind of measuring tool or go/no-go devices.		
		Category Subtotal			
		Set in Order / Straighten Score: Subtotal divided by 6			
SHINE / SWEEP	XIII	The storage of gauges and tooling.	Arrangement of all fixtures, tools, and attachments are kept in clean area for storage and no risk of damage during transporting to storage.		
	XIV	Clear when equipment needs maintenance and when last maintained.	Buttons and switches on machinery marked, highlighted, and labeled. Check sheets clean and displayed. Maintenance is scheduled; levels of fluids, lubrication of joints are clearly itemized and illustrated.		
	XV	Assess the cleanliness of the work zone.	How dust free are the areas. Look under desks and behind work spaces to see if there is garbage and other unnecessary items.		
	XVI	Safety of the equipment, are areas gated off and safe for workers?	Spray shields and physical guards are in active use to keep items and liquids getting on the floor. Areas that are critical are clearly marked to protect workers.		
	XVII	Assess status of equipment in the area. Cleanliness overall appearance.	Are machines and equipment known to be on a schedule of cleaning?		
		Category Subtotal			
		Shine / Sweep Score: Subtotal divided by 5			
STANDARDIZE	XVIII	Is there visual color diagramming and color coding?	A clear and present color coding system is present in the work zone and across the company. It is clear that standards are being maintained and improved on.		
	XIX	Assess the access ways in case of emergency.	All emergency systems; fire vehicles, fire extinguishers, and emergency equipment free of obstruction and clear at all times. Access to electrical controls and fuses are known, marked, and free of any obstructions.		
	XX	The aisle ways are bright with light and clearly marked.	Walkways are clearly highlighted for direction, aisle access identified at any moment while in the work zone.		
	XXI	General area has quantity limits for materials and are marked clearly.	Heights are marked, quantity of materials are known, and min vs. max.		
	XXII	Is there clear document control of information in the work zone?	All information and documentation is controlled, labeled, and revisions are up to date. There are no label-less binders or pieces of paper in the area.		
		Category Subtotal			
		Standardize Score: Subtotal divided by 5			
SUSTAIN	XXIII	The aisle ways are clean and maintenance is clear.	Aisles are never full of anything and are clear for passage. All items and products not stored in the aisle and storage is next to aisle accessible for transportation.		
	XXIV	Illustrations and work zone plans are available to compare against.	5S has a maintenance system that allows for control of change and improvement of 5S in the work zones. Scoring is kept on each of these items and history is present and visible to support future improvement.		
	XXV	Ability for tools to be set back in place of storage.	No self-discipline is necessary to ensure that all tools, dies, jigs, and equipment are put back in the same spot. The effort of putting back should not require organizational skills.		
	XXVI	Evaluate the involvement of supervisors in 5S.	Supervisors are actively involved in the review process of 5S and are supporting improvement activities of the work areas.		
		Category Subtotal			
		Sustain Score: Subtotal divided by 4			**Total "Category Subtotals" divide by 26 average 5S score: TOTAL**

5S Evaluation Review

Date: _____   Evaluation Area:_____

5S Element	Number	Evaluation Criteria	Rank these items from 1 through 5: 5 being well done	Score (1-5)	Ideas / Suggestions / Comments
SORT	I	Are the aisles and walkways open and clear?	All items that are not necessary or unsafe have been removed from the area where people travel and work.		
	II	Is the work zone free of any spills of fluids?	Consider whether there are any chemicals, lubricants, water, oils or other materials that may be hazardous in the area and on the floor.		
	III	Is the work zone free of unnecessary articles and items?	Are items that are not needed been removed from the work zone, i.e. tools, jigs, stationary, extra items.		
	IV	Is the work zone free of excess consumables/materials?	Evaluate against how many items are in the production work zone. Assess if the materials, parts, and supplies are currently needed for operations.		
	V	Is the information board active?	All announcements are displayed currently and in good presentable shape. Arrangement is straight and placed under appropriate headings.		
	VI	Are the areas walls and dividers free of items not used in operations?	Extra items are not on the walls, dividers, or hanging of signs that are not necessary.		
			Category Subtotal		
			Sort Score: Subtotal divided by 6		
SET IN ORDER / STRAIGHTEN	VII	Evaluate any documentation storage.	Only documents to do the job are stored at the work zone. These documents are stored nicely and in an orderly fashion that is recognizable to outsiders.		
	VIII	How are the shelves, desks, and work surfaces arranged?	All locations of items are labeled, marked, and it is known if they are missing.		
	IX	How are the tools and material used in operations stored?	No items are resting on walls or tucked in corners. No items are resting on equipment, cupboards, or other fixtures.		
	X	Evaluate container and packaging locations and tidiness.	Materials, boxes, storage containers, and other items are stored in the appropriate place and orientated well for operations. Also, they are secure and not causing any danger to the workforce.		
	XI	Assess order and where items are found on the floor.	Nothing is sitting directly on the floor and no materials are left around the area. Items that need to be on the floor are clearly marked and positioned in designated areas clearly outlined on the floor.		
	XII	Easiness to access the tools for machines and measuring gauges.	Materials, tools, jigs, attachments, and fixtures are organized so that they are all easily within reach of the operator. Consider this as well for any kind of measuring tool or go/no-go devices.		
			Category Subtotal		
			Set in Order / Straighten Score: Subtotal divided by 6		
SHINE / SWEEP	XIII	The storage of gauges and tooling.	Arrangement of all fixtures, tools, and attachments are kept in clean area for storage and no risk of damage during transporting to storage.		
	XIV	Clear when equipment needs maintenance and when last maintained.	Buttons and switches on machinery marked, highlighted, and labeled. Check sheets clean and displayed. Maintenance is scheduled; levels of fluids, lubrication of joints are clearly itemized and illustrated.		
	XV	Assess the cleanliness of the work zone.	How dust free are the areas. Look under desks and behind work spaces to see if there is garbage and other unnecessary items.		
	XVI	Safety of the equipment, are areas gated off and safe for workers?	Spray shields and physical guards are in active use to keep items and liquids getting on the floor. Areas that are critical are clearly marked to protect workers.		
	XVII	Assess status of equipment in the area. Cleanliness overall appearance.	Are machines and equipment known to be on a schedule of cleaning?		
			Category Subtotal		
			Shine / Sweep Score: Subtotal divided by 5		
STANDARDIZE	XVIII	Is there visual color diagramming and color coding?	A clear and present color coding system is present in the work zone and across the company. It is clear that standards are being maintained and improved on.		
	XIX	Assess the access ways in case of emergency.	All emergency systems; fire vehicles, fire extinguishers, and emergency equipment free of obstruction and clear at all times. Access to electrical controls and fuses are known, marked, and free of any obstructions.		
	XX	The aisle ways are bright with light and clearly marked.	Walkways are clearly highlighted for direction, aisle access identified at any moment while in the work zone.		
	XXI	General area has quantity limits for materials and are marked clearly.	Heights are marked, quantity of materials are known, and min vs. max.		
	XXII	Is there clear document control of information in the work zone?	All information and documentation is controlled, labeled, and revisions are up to date. There are no label-less binders or pieces of paper in the area.		
			Category Subtotal		
			Standardize Score: Subtotal divided by 5		
SUSTAIN	XXIII	The aisle ways are clean and maintenance is clear.	Aisles are never full of anything and are clear for passage. All items and products not stored in the aisle and storage is next to aisle accessible for transportation.		
	XXIV	Illustrations and work zone plans are available to compare against.	5S has a maintenance system that allows for control of change and improvement of 5S in the work zones. Scoring is kept on each of these items and history is present and visible to support future improvement.		
	XXV	Ability for tools to be set back in place of storage.	No self-discipline is necessary to ensure that all tools, dies, jigs, and equipment are put back in the same spot. The effort of putting back should not require organizational skills.		
	XXVI	Evaluate the involvement of supervisors in 5S.	Supervisors are actively involved in the review process of 5S and are supporting improvement activities of the work areas.		
			Category Subtotal		
			Sustain Score: Subtotal divided by 4		

Total "Category Subtotals" divide by 26 average 5S score: TOTAL

5S Evaluation Review

Date: _____   Evaluation Area: _____

5S Element	Number	Evaluation Criteria	Rank these items from 1 through 5: 5 being well done	Score (1-5)	Ideas / Suggestions / Comments
SORT	I	Are the aisles and walkways open and clear?	All items that are not necessary or unsafe have been removed from the area where people travel and work.		
	II	Is the work zone free of any spills of fluids?	Consider whether there are any chemicals, lubricants, water, oils or other materials that may be hazardous in the area and on the floor.		
	III	Is the work zone free of unnecessary articles and items?	Are items that are not needed been removed from the work zone, i.e. tools, jigs, stationary, extra items.		
	IV	Is the work zone free of excess consumables/materials?	Evaluate against how many items are in the production work zone. Assess if the materials, parts, and supplies are currently needed for operations.		
	V	Is the information board active?	All announcements are displayed currently and in good presentable shape. Arrangement is straight and placed under appropriate headings.		
	VI	Are the areas walls and dividers free of items not used in operations?	Extra items are not on the walls, dividers, or hanging of signs that are not necessary.		
		Category Subtotal			
		Sort Score: Subtotal divided by 6			
SET IN ORDER / STRAIGHTEN	VII	Evaluate any documentation storage.	Only documents to do the job are stored at the work zone. These documents are stored nicely and in an orderly fashion that is recognizable to outsiders.		
	VIII	How are the shelves, desks, and work surfaces arranged?	All locations of items are labeled, marked, and it is known if they are missing.		
	IX	How are the tools and material used in operations stored?	No items are resting on walls or tucked in corners. No items are resting on equipment, cupboards, or other fixtures.		
	X	Evaluate container and packaging locations and tidiness.	Materials, boxes, storage containers, and other items are stored in the appropriate place and orientated well for operations. Also, they are secure and not causing any danger to the workforce.		
	XI	Assess order and where items are found on the floor.	Nothing is sitting directly on the floor and no materials are left around the area. Items that need to be on the floor are clearly marked and positioned in designated areas clearly outlined on the floor.		
	XII	Easiness to access the tools for machines and measuring gauges.	Materials, tools, jigs, attachments, and fixtures are organized so that they are all easily within reach of the operator. Consider this as well for any kind of measuring tool or go/no-go devices.		
		Category Subtotal			
		Set in Order / Straighten Score: Subtotal divided by 6			
SHINE / SWEEP	XIII	The storage of gauges and tooling.	Arrangement of all fixtures, tools, and attachments are kept in clean area for storage and no risk of damage during transporting to storage.		
	XIV	Clear when equipment needs maintenance and when last maintained.	Buttons and switches on machinery marked, highlighted, and labeled. Check sheets clean and displayed. Maintenance is scheduled; levels of fluids, lubrication of joints are clearly itemized and illustrated.		
	XV	Assess the cleanliness of the work zone.	How dust free are the areas. Look under desks and behind work spaces to see if there is garbage and other unnecessary items.		
	XVI	Safety of the equipment, are areas gated off and safe for workers?	Spray shields and physical guards are in active use to keep items and liquids getting on the floor. Areas that are critical are clearly marked to protect workers.		
	XVII	Assess status of equipment in the area. Cleanliness overall appearance.	Are machines and equipment known to be on a schedule of cleaning?		
		Category Subtotal			
		Shine / Sweep Score: Subtotal divided by 5			
STANDARDIZE	XVIII	Is there visual color diagramming and color coding?	A clear and present color coding system is present in the work zone and across the company. It is clear that standards are being maintained and improved on.		
	XIX	Assess the access ways in case of emergency.	All emergency systems; fire vehicles, fire extinguishers, and emergency equipment free of obstruction and clear at all times. Access to electrical controls and fuses are known, marked, and free of any obstructions.		
	XX	The aisle ways are bright with light and clearly marked.	Walkways are clearly highlighted for direction, aisle access identified at any moment while in the work zone.		
	XXI	General area has quantity limits for materials and are marked clearly.	Heights are marked, quantity of materials are known, and min vs. max.		
	XXII	Is there clear document control of information in the work zone?	All information and documentation is controlled, labeled, and revisions are up to date. There are no label-less binders or pieces of paper in the area.		
		Category Subtotal			
		Standardize Score: Subtotal divided by 5			
SUSTAIN	XXIII	The aisle ways are clean and maintenance is clear.	Aisles are never full of anything and are clear for passage. All items and products not stored in the aisle and storage is next to aisle accessible for transportation.		
	XXIV	Illustrations and work zone plans are available to compare against.	5S has a maintenance system that allows for control of change and improvement of 5S in the work zones. Scoring is kept on each of these items and history is present and visible to support future improvement.		
	XXV	Ability for tools to be set back in place of storage.	No self-discipline is necessary to ensure that all tools, dies, jigs, and equipment are put back in the same spot. The effort of putting back should not require organizational skills.		
	XXVI	Evaluate the involvement of supervisors in 5S.	Supervisors are actively involved in the review process of 5S and are supporting improvement activities of the work areas.		
		Category Subtotal			
		Sustain Score: Subtotal divided by 4		**Total "Category Subtotals" divide by 26 average 5S score: TOTAL**	

5S Evaluation Review

Date: _____   Evaluation Area: _____

5S Element	Number	Evaluation Criteria	Rank these items from 1 through 5: 5 being well done	Score (1-5)	Ideas / Suggestions / Comments
SORT	I	Are the aisles and walkways open and clear?	All items that are not necessary or unsafe have been removed from the area where people travel and work.		
	II	Is the work zone free of any spills of fluids?	Consider whether there are any chemicals, lubricants, water, oils or other materials that may be hazardous in the area and on the floor.		
	III	Is the work zone free of unnecessary articles and items?	Are items that are not needed been removed from the work zone, i.e. tools, jigs, stationary, extra items.		
	IV	Is the work zone free of excess consumables/materials?	Evaluate against how many items are in the production work zone. Assess if the materials, parts, and supplies are currently needed for operations.		
	V	Is the information board active?	All announcements are displayed currently and in good presentable shape. Arrangement is straight and placed under appropriate headings.		
	VI	Are the areas walls and dividers free of items not used in operations?	Extra items are not on the walls, dividers, or hanging of signs that are not necessary.		
		Category Subtotal			
		Sort Score: Subtotal divided by 6			
SET IN ORDER / STRAIGHTEN	VII	Evaluate any documentation storage.	Only documents to do the job are stored at the work zone. These documents are stored nicely and in an orderly fashion that is recognizable to outsiders.		
	VIII	How are the shelves, desks, and work surfaces arranged?	All locations of items are labeled, marked, and it is known if they are missing.		
	IX	How are the tools and material used in operations stored?	No items are resting on walls or tucked in corners. No items are resting on equipment, cupboards, or other fixtures.		
	X	Evaluate container and packaging locations and tidiness.	Materials, boxes, storage containers, and other items are stored in the appropriate place and orientated well for operations. Also, they are secure and not causing any danger to the workforce.		
	XI	Assess order and where items are found on the floor.	Nothing is sitting directly on the floor and no materials are left around the area. Items that need to be on the floor are clearly marked and positioned in designated areas clearly outlined on the floor.		
	XII	Easiness to access the tools for machines and measuring gauges.	Materials, tools, jigs, attachments, and fixtures are organized so that they are all easily within reach of the operator. Consider this as well for any kind of measuring tool or go/no-go devices.		
		Category Subtotal			
		Set in Order / Straighten Score: Subtotal divided by 6			
SHINE / SWEEP	XIII	The storage of gauges and tooling.	Arrangement of all fixtures, tools, and attachments are kept in clean area for storage and no risk of damage during transporting to storage.		
	XIV	Clear when equipment needs maintenance and when last maintained.	Buttons and switches on machinery marked, highlighted, and labeled. Check sheets clean and displayed. Maintenance is scheduled; levels of fluids, lubrication of joints are clearly itemized and illustrated.		
	XV	Assess the cleanliness of the work zone.	How dust free are the areas. Look under desks and behind work spaces to see if there is garbage and other unnecessary items.		
	XVI	Safety of the equipment, are areas gated off and safe for workers?	Spray shields and physical guards are in active use to keep items and liquids getting on the floor. Areas that are critical are clearly marked to protect workers.		
	XVII	Assess status of equipment in the area. Cleanliness overall appearance.	Are machines and equipment known to be on a schedule of cleaning?		
		Category Subtotal			
		Shine / Sweep Score: Subtotal divided by 5			
STANDARDIZE	XVIII	Is there visual color diagramming and color coding?	A clear and present color coding system is present in the work zone and across the company. It is clear that standards are being maintained and improved on.		
	XIX	Assess the access ways in case of emergency.	All emergency systems; fire vehicles, fire extinguishers, and emergency equipment free of obstruction and clear at all times. Access to electrical controls and fuses are known, marked, and free of any obstructions.		
	XX	The aisle ways are bright with light and clearly marked.	Walkways are clearly highlighted for direction, aisle access identified at any moment while in the work zone.		
	XXI	General area has quantity limits for materials and are marked clearly.	Heights are marked, quantity of materials are known, and min vs. max.		
	XXII	Is there clear document control of information in the work zone?	All information and documentation is controlled, labeled, and revisions are up to date. There are no label-less binders or pieces of paper in the area.		
		Category Subtotal			
		Standardize Score: Subtotal divided by 5			
SUSTAIN	XXIII	The aisle ways are clean and maintenance is clear.	Aisles are never full of anything and are clear for passage. All items and products not stored in the aisle and storage is next to aisle accessible for transportation.		
	XXIV	Illustrations and work zone plans are available to compare against.	5S has a maintenance system that allows for control of change and improvement of 5S in the work zones. Scoring is kept on each of these items and history is present and visible to support future improvement.		
	XXV	Ability for tools to be set back in place of storage.	No self-discipline is necessary to ensure that all tools, dies, jigs, and equipment are put back in the same spot. The effort of putting back should not require organizational skills.		
	XXVI	Evaluate the involvement of supervisors in 5S.	Supervisors are actively involved in the review process of 5S and are supporting improvement activities of the work areas.		
		Category Subtotal			
		Sustain Score: Subtotal divided by 4			**Total "Category Subtotals" divide by 26 average 5S score: TOTAL**

5S Evaluation Review

Date: _____   Evaluation Area: _____

5S Element	Number	Evaluation Criteria	Rank these items from 1 through 5: 5 being well done	Score (1-5)	Ideas / Suggestions / Comments
SORT	I	Are the aisles and walkways open and clear?	All items that are not necessary or unsafe have been removed from the area where people travel and work.		
	II	Is the work zone free of any spills of fluids?	Consider whether there are any chemicals, lubricants, water, oils or other materials that may be hazardous in the area and on the floor.		
	III	Is the work zone free of unnecessary articles and items?	Are items that are not needed been removed from the work zone, i.e. tools, jigs, stationary, extra items.		
	IV	Is the work zone free of excess consumables/materials?	Evaluate against how many items are in the production work zone. Assess if the materials, parts, and supplies are currently needed for operations.		
	V	Is the information board active?	All announcements are displayed currently and in good presentable shape. Arrangement is straight and placed under appropriate headings.		
	VI	Are the areas walls and dividers free of items not used in operations?	Extra items are not on the walls, dividers, or hanging of signs that are not necessary.		
			Category Subtotal		
			Sort Score: Subtotal divided by 6		
SET IN ORDER / STRAIGHTEN	VII	Evaluate any documentation storage.	Only documents to do the job are stored at the work zone. These documents are stored nicely and in an orderly fashion that is recognizable to outsiders.		
	VIII	How are the shelves, desks, and work surfaces arranged?	All locations of items are labeled, marked, and it is known if they are missing.		
	IX	How are the tools and material used in operations stored?	No items are resting on walls or tucked in corners. No items are resting on equipment, cupboards, or other fixtures.		
	X	Evaluate container and packaging locations and tidiness.	Materials, boxes, storage containers, and other items are stored in the appropriate place and orientated well for operations. Also, they are secure and not causing any danger to the workforce.		
	XI	Assess order and where items are found on the floor.	Nothing is sitting directly on the floor and no materials are left around the area. Items that need to be on the floor are clearly marked and positioned in designated areas clearly outlined on the floor.		
	XII	Easiness to access the tools for machines and measuring gauges.	Materials, tools, jigs, attachments, and fixtures are organized so that they are all easily within reach of the operator. Consider this as well for any kind of measuring tool or go/no-go devices.		
			Category Subtotal		
			Set in Order / Straighten Score: Subtotal divided by 6		
SHINE / SWEEP	XIII	The storage of gauges and tooling.	Arrangement of all fixtures, tools, and attachments are kept in clean area for storage and no risk of damage during transporting to storage.		
	XIV	Clear when equipment needs maintenance and when last maintained.	Buttons and switches on machinery marked, highlighted, and labeled. Check sheets clean and displayed. Maintenance is scheduled; levels of fluids, lubrication of joints are clearly itemized and illustrated.		
	XV	Assess the cleanliness of the work zone.	How dust free are the areas. Look under desks and behind work spaces to see if there is garbage and other unnecessary items.		
	XVI	Safety of the equipment, are areas gated off and safe for workers?	Spray shields and physical guards are in active use to keep items and liquids getting on the floor. Areas that are critical are clearly marked to protect workers.		
	XVII	Assess status of equipment in the area. Cleanliness overall appearance.	Are machines and equipment known to be on a schedule of cleaning?		
			Category Subtotal		
			Shine / Sweep Score: Subtotal divided by 5		
STANDARDIZE	XVIII	Is there visual color diagramming and color coding?	A clear and present color coding system is present in the work zone and across the company. It is clear that standards are being maintained and improved on.		
	XIX	Assess the access ways in case of emergency.	All emergency systems; fire vehicles, fire extinguishers, and emergency equipment free of obstruction and clear at all times. Access to electrical controls and fuses are known, marked, and free of any obstructions.		
	XX	The aisle ways are bright with light and clearly marked.	Walkways are clearly highlighted for direction, aisle access identified at any moment while in the work zone.		
	XXI	General area has quantity limits for materials and are marked clearly.	Heights are marked, quantity of materials are known, and min vs. max.		
	XXII	Is there clear document control of information in the work zone?	All information and documentation is controlled, labeled, and revisions are up to date. There are no label-less binders or pieces of paper in the area.		
			Category Subtotal		
			Standardize Score: Subtotal divided by 5		
SUSTAIN	XXIII	The aisle ways are clean and maintenance is clear.	Aisles are never full of anything and are clear for passage. All items and products not stored in the aisle and storage is next to aisle accessible for transportation.		
	XXIV	Illustrations and work zone plans are available to compare against.	5S has a maintenance system that allows for control of change and improvement of 5S in the work zones. Scoring is kept on each of these items and history is present and visible to support future improvement.		
	XXV	Ability for tools to be set back in place of storage.	No self-discipline is necessary to ensure that all tools, dies, jigs, and equipment are put back in the same spot. The effort of putting back should not require organizational skills.		
	XXVI	Evaluate the involvement of supervisors in 5S.	Supervisors are actively involved in the review process of 5S and are supporting improvement activities of the work areas.		
			Category Subtotal		
			Sustain Score: Subtotal divided by 4		
			Total "Category Subtotals" divide by 26 average 5S score: TOTAL		

5S Evaluation Review

Date: _____   Evaluation Area: _____

5S Element	Number	Evaluation Criteria	Rank these items from 1 through 5: 5 being well done	Score (1-5)	Ideas / Suggestions / Comments
SORT	I	Are the aisles and walkways open and clear?	All items that are not necessary or unsafe have been removed from the area where people travel and work.		
	II	Is the work zone free of any spills of fluids?	Consider whether there are any chemicals, lubricants, water, oils or other materials that may be hazardous in the area and on the floor.		
	III	Is the work zone free of unnecessary articles and items?	Are items that are not needed been removed from the work zone, i.e. tools, jigs, stationary, extra items.		
	IV	Is the work zone free of excess consumables/materials?	Evaluate against how many items are in the production work zone. Assess if the materials, parts, and supplies are currently needed for operations.		
	V	Is the information board active?	All announcements are displayed currently and in good presentable shape. Arrangement is straight and placed under appropriate headings.		
	VI	Are the areas walls and dividers free of items not used in operations?	Extra items are not on the walls, dividers, or hanging of signs that are not necessary.		
			Category Subtotal		
			Sort Score: Subtotal divided by 6		
SET IN ORDER / STRAIGHTEN	VII	Evaluate any documentation storage.	Only documents to do the job are stored at the work zone. These documents are stored nicely and in an orderly fashion that is recognizable to outsiders.		
	VIII	How are the shelves, desks, and work surfaces arranged?	All locations of items are labeled, marked, and it is known if they are missing.		
	IX	How are the tools and material used in operations stored?	No items are resting on walls or tucked in corners. No items are resting on equipment, cupboards, or other fixtures.		
	X	Evaluate container and packaging locations and tidiness.	Materials, boxes, storage containers, and other items are stored in the appropriate place and orientated well for operations. Also, they are secure and not causing any danger to the workforce.		
	XI	Assess order and where items are found on the floor.	Nothing is sitting directly on the floor and no materials are left around the area. Items that need to be on the floor are clearly marked and positioned in designated areas clearly outlined on the floor.		
	XII	Easiness to access the tools for machines and measuring gauges.	Materials, tools, jigs, attachments, and fixtures are organized so that they are all easily within reach of the operator. Consider this as well for any kind of measuring tool or go/no-go devices.		
			Category Subtotal		
			Set in Order / Straighten Score: Subtotal divided by 6		
SHINE / SWEEP	XIII	The storage of gauges and tooling.	Arrangement of all fixtures, tools, and attachments are kept in clean area for storage and no risk of damage during transporting to storage.		
	XIV	Clear when equipment needs maintenance and when last maintained.	Buttons and switches on machinery marked, highlighted, and labeled. Check sheets clean and displayed. Maintenance is scheduled; levels of fluids, lubrication of joints are clearly itemized and illustrated.		
	XV	Assess the cleanliness of the work zone.	How dust free are the areas. Look under desks and behind work spaces to see if there is garbage and other unnecessary items.		
	XVI	Safety of the equipment, are areas gated off and safe for workers?	Spray shields and physical guards are in active use to keep items and liquids getting on the floor. Areas that are critical are clearly marked to protect workers.		
	XVII	Assess status of equipment in the area. Cleanliness overall appearance.	Are machines and equipment known to be on a schedule of cleaning?		
			Category Subtotal		
			Shine / Sweep Score: Subtotal divided by 5		
STANDARDIZE	XVIII	Is there visual color diagramming and color coding?	A clear and present color coding system is present in the work zone and across the company. It is clear that standards are being maintained and improved on.		
	XIX	Assess the access ways in case of emergency.	All emergency systems; fire vehicles, fire extinguishers, and emergency equipment free of obstruction and clear at all times. Access to electrical controls and fuses are known, marked, and free of any obstructions.		
	XX	The aisle ways are bright with light and clearly marked.	Walkways are clearly highlighted for direction, aisle access identified at any moment while in the work zone.		
	XXI	General area has quantity limits for materials and are marked clearly.	Heights are marked, quantity of materials are known, and min vs. max.		
	XXII	Is there clear document control of information in the work zone?	All information and documentation is controlled, labeled, and revisions are up to date. There are no label-less binders or pieces of paper in the area.		
			Category Subtotal		
			Standardize Score: Subtotal divided by 5		
SUSTAIN	XXIII	The aisle ways are clean and maintenance is clear.	Aisles are never full of anything and are clear for passage. All items and products not stored in the aisle and storage is next to aisle accessible for transportation.		
	XXIV	Illustrations and work zone plans are available to compare against.	5S has a maintenance system that allows for control of change and improvement of 5S in the work zones. Scoring is kept on each of these items and history is present and visible to support future improvement.		
	XXV	Ability for tools to be set back in place of storage.	No self-discipline is necessary to ensure that all tools, dies, jigs, and equipment are put back in the same spot. The effort of putting back should not require organizational skills.		
	XXVI	Evaluate the involvement of supervisors in 5S.	Supervisors are actively involved in the review process of 5S and are supporting improvement activities of the work areas.		
			Category Subtotal		
			Sustain Score: Subtotal divided by 4		**Total "Category Subtotals" divide by 26 average 5S score: TOTAL**

5S Evaluation Review

Date: _____   Evaluation Area: _____

5S Element	Number	Evaluation Criteria	Rank these items from 1 through 5: 5 being well done	Score (1-5)	Ideas / Suggestions / Comments
SORT	I	Are the aisles and walkways open and clear?	All items that are not necessary or unsafe have been removed from the area where people travel and work.		
	II	Is the work zone free of any spills of fluids?	Consider whether there are any chemicals, lubricants, water, oils or other materials that may be hazardous in the area and on the floor.		
	III	Is the work zone free of unnecessary articles and items?	Are items that are not needed been removed from the work zone, i.e. tools, jigs, stationary, extra items.		
	IV	Is the work zone free of excess consumables/materials?	Evaluate against how many items are in the production work zone. Assess if the materials, parts, and supplies are currently needed for operations.		
	V	Is the information board active?	All announcements are displayed currently and in good presentable shape. Arrangement is straight and placed under appropriate headings.		
	VI	Are the areas walls and dividers free of items not used in operations?	Extra items are not on the walls, dividers, or hanging of signs that are not necessary.		
			Category Subtotal		
			Sort Score: Subtotal divided by 6		
SET IN ORDER / STRAIGHTEN	VII	Evaluate any documentation storage.	Only documents to do the job are stored at the work zone. These documents are stored nicely and in an orderly fashion that is recognizable to outsiders.		
	VIII	How are the shelves, desks, and work surfaces arranged?	All locations of items are labeled, marked, and it is known if they are missing.		
	IX	How are the tools and material used in operations stored?	No items are resting on walls or tucked in corners. No items are resting on equipment, cupboards, or other fixtures.		
	X	Evaluate container and packaging locations and tidiness.	Materials, boxes, storage containers, and other items are stored in the appropriate place and orientated well for operations. Also, they are secure and not causing any danger to the workforce.		
	XI	Assess order and where items are found on the floor.	Nothing is sitting directly on the floor and no materials are left around the area. Items that need to be on the floor are clearly marked and positioned in designated areas clearly outlined on the floor.		
	XII	Easiness to access the tools for machines and measuring gauges.	Materials, tools, jigs, attachments, and fixtures are organized so that they are all easily within reach of the operator. Consider this as well for any kind of measuring tool or go/no-go devices.		
			Category Subtotal		
			Set in Order / Straighten Score: Subtotal divided by 6		
SHINE / SWEEP	XIII	The storage of gauges and tooling.	Arrangement of all fixtures, tools, and attachments are kept in clean area for storage and no risk of damage during transporting to storage.		
	XIV	Clear when equipment needs maintenance and when last maintained.	Buttons and switches on machinery marked, highlighted, and labeled. Check sheets clean and displayed. Maintenance is scheduled; levels of fluids, lubrication of joints are clearly itemized and illustrated.		
	XV	Assess the cleanliness of the work zone.	How dust free are the areas. Look under desks and behind work spaces to see if there is garbage and other unnecessary items.		
	XVI	Safety of the equipment, are areas gated off and safe for workers?	Spray shields and physical guards are in active use to keep items and liquids getting on the floor. Areas that are critical are clearly marked to protect workers.		
	XVII	Assess status of equipment in the area. Cleanliness overall appearance.	Are machines and equipment known to be on a schedule of cleaning?		
			Category Subtotal		
			Shine / Sweep Score: Subtotal divided by 5		
STANDARDIZE	XVIII	Is there visual color diagramming and color coding?	A clear and present color coding system is present in the work zone and across the company. It is clear that standards are being maintained and improved on.		
	XIX	Assess the access ways in case of emergency.	All emergency systems; fire vehicles, fire extinguishers, and emergency equipment free of obstruction and clear at all times. Access to electrical controls and fuses are known, marked, and free of any obstructions.		
	XX	The aisle ways are bright with light and clearly marked.	Walkways are clearly highlighted for direction, aisle access identified at any moment while in the work zone.		
	XXI	General area has quantity limits for materials and are marked clearly.	Heights are marked, quantity of materials are known, and min vs. max.		
	XXII	Is there clear document control of information in the work zone?	All information and documentation is controlled, labeled, and revisions are up to date. There are no label-less binders or pieces of paper in the area.		
			Category Subtotal		
			Standardize Score: Subtotal divided by 5		
SUSTAIN	XXIII	The aisle ways are clean and maintenance is clear.	Aisles are never full of anything and are clear for passage. All items and products not stored in the aisle and storage is next to aisle accessible for transportation.		
	XXIV	Illustrations and work zone plans are available to compare against.	5S has a maintenance system that allows for control of change and improvement of 5S in the work zones. Scoring is kept on each of these items and history is present and visible to support future improvement.		
	XXV	Ability for tools to be set back in place of storage.	No self-discipline is necessary to ensure that all tools, dies, jigs, and equipment are put back in the same spot. The effort of putting back should not require organizational skills.		
	XXVI	Evaluate the involvement of supervisors in 5S.	Supervisors are actively involved in the review process of 5S and are supporting improvement activities of the work areas.		
			Category Subtotal		
			Sustain Score: Subtotal divided by 4		**Total "Category Subtotals" divide by 26 average 5S score: TOTAL**

5S Evaluation Review

Date: _____   Evaluation Area: _____

5S Element	Number	Evaluation Criteria	Rank these items from 1 through 5: 5 being well done	Score (1-5)	Ideas / Suggestions / Comments
SORT	I	Are the aisles and walkways open and clear?	All items that are not necessary or unsafe have been removed from the area where people travel and work.		
	II	Is the work zone free of any spills of fluids?	Consider whether there are any chemicals, lubricants, water, oils or other materials that may be hazardous in the area and on the floor.		
	III	Is the work zone free of unnecessary articles and items?	Are items that are not needed been removed from the work zone, i.e. tools, jigs, stationary, extra items.		
	IV	Is the work zone free of excess consumables/materials?	Evaluate against how many items are in the production work zone. Assess if the materials, parts, and supplies are currently needed for operations.		
	V	Is the information board active?	All announcements are displayed currently and in good presentable shape. Arrangement is straight and placed under appropriate headings.		
	VI	Are the areas walls and dividers free of items not used in operations?	Extra items are not on the walls, dividers, or hanging of signs that are not necessary.		
			Category Subtotal		
			Sort Score: Subtotal divided by 6		
SET IN ORDER / STRAIGHTEN	VII	Evaluate any documentation storage.	Only documents to do the job are stored at the work zone. These documents are stored nicely and in an orderly fashion that is recognizable to outsiders.		
	VIII	How are the shelves, desks, and work surfaces arranged?	All locations of items are labeled, marked, and it is known if they are missing.		
	IX	How are the tools and material used in operations stored?	No items are resting on walls or tucked in corners. No items are resting on equipment, cupboards, or other fixtures.		
	X	Evaluate container and packaging locations and tidiness.	Materials, boxes, storage containers, and other items are stored in the appropriate place and orientated well for operations. Also, they are secure and not causing any danger to the workforce.		
	XI	Assess order and where items are found on the floor.	Nothing is sitting directly on the floor and no materials are left around the area. Items that need to be on the floor are clearly marked and positioned in designated areas clearly outlined on the floor.		
	XII	Easiness to access the tools for machines and measuring gauges.	Materials, tools, jigs, attachments, and fixtures are organized so that they are all easily within reach of the operator. Consider this as well for any kind of measuring tool or go/no-go devices.		
			Category Subtotal		
			Set in Order / Straighten Score: Subtotal divided by 6		
SHINE / SWEEP	XIII	The storage of gauges and tooling.	Arrangement of all fixtures, tools, and attachments are kept in clean area for storage and no risk of damage during transporting to storage.		
	XIV	Clear when equipment needs maintenance and when last maintained.	Buttons and switches on machinery marked, highlighted, and labeled. Check sheets clean and displayed. Maintenance is scheduled; levels of fluids, lubrication of joints are clearly itemized and illustrated.		
	XV	Assess the cleanliness of the work zone.	How dust free are the areas. Look under desks and behind work spaces to see if there is garbage and other unnecessary items.		
	XVI	Safety of the equipment, are areas gated off and safe for workers?	Spray shields and physical guards are in active use to keep items and liquids getting on the floor. Areas that are critical are clearly marked to protect workers.		
	XVII	Assess status of equipment in the area. Cleanliness overall appearance.	Are machines and equipment known to be on a schedule of cleaning?		
			Category Subtotal		
			Shine / Sweep Score: Subtotal divided by 5		
STANDARDIZE	XVIII	Is there visual color diagramming and color coding?	A clear and present color coding system is present in the work zone and across the company. It is clear that standards are being maintained and improved on.		
	XIX	Assess the access ways in case of emergency.	All emergency systems; fire vehicles, fire extinguishers, and emergency equipment free of obstruction and clear at all times. Access to electrical controls and fuses are known, marked, and free of any obstructions.		
	XX	The aisle ways are bright with light and clearly marked.	Walkways are clearly highlighted for direction, aisle access identified at any moment while in the work zone.		
	XXI	General area has quantity limits for materials and are marked clearly.	Heights are marked, quantity of materials are known, and min vs. max.		
	XXII	Is there clear document control of information in the work zone?	All information and documentation is controlled, labeled, and revisions are up to date. There are no label-less binders or pieces of paper in the area.		
			Category Subtotal		
			Standardize Score: Subtotal divided by 5		
SUSTAIN	XXIII	The aisle ways are clean and maintenance is clear.	Aisles are never full of anything and are clear for passage. All items and products not stored in the aisle and storage is next to aisle accessible for transportation.		
	XXIV	Illustrations and work zone plans are available to compare against.	5S has a maintenance system that allows for control of change and improvement of 5S in the work zones. Scoring is kept on each of these items and history is present and visible to support future improvement.		
	XXV	Ability for tools to be set back in place of storage.	No self-discipline is necessary to ensure that all tools, dies, jigs, and equipment are put back in the same spot. The effort of putting back should not require organizational skills.		
	XXVI	Evaluate the involvement of supervisors in 5S.	Supervisors are actively involved in the review process of 5S and are supporting improvement activities of the work areas.		
			Category Subtotal		
			Sustain Score: Subtotal divided by 4		**Total "Category Subtotals" divide by 26 average 5S score: TOTAL**

5S Evaluation Review

Date: _____   Evaluation Area:_____

5S Element	Number	Evaluation Criteria	Rank these items from 1 through 5: 5 being well done	Score (1-5)	Ideas / Suggestions / Comments
SORT	I	Are the aisles and walkways open and clear?	All items that are not necessary or unsafe have been removed from the area where people travel and work.		
	II	Is the work zone free of any spills of fluids?	Consider whether there are any chemicals, lubricants, water, oils or other materials that may be hazardous in the area and on the floor.		
	III	Is the work zone free of unnecessary articles and items?	Are items that are not needed been removed from the work zone, i.e. tools, jigs, stationary, extra items.		
	IV	Is the work zone free of excess consumables/materials?	Evaluate against how many items are in the production work zone. Assess if the materials, parts, and supplies are currently needed for operations.		
	V	Is the information board active?	All announcements are displayed currently and in good presentable shape. Arrangement is straight and placed under appropriate headings.		
	VI	Are the areas walls and dividers free of items not used in operations?	Extra items are not on the walls, dividers, or hanging of signs that are not necessary.		
		Category Subtotal			
		Sort Score: Subtotal divided by 6			
SET IN ORDER / STRAIGHTEN	VII	Evaluate any documentation storage.	Only documents to do the job are stored at the work zone. These documents are stored nicely and in an orderly fashion that is recognizable to outsiders.		
	VIII	How are the shelves, desks, and work surfaces arranged?	All locations of items are labeled, marked, and it is known if they are missing.		
	IX	How are the tools and material used in operations stored?	No items are resting on walls or tucked in corners. No items are resting on equipment, cupboards, or other fixtures.		
	X	Evaluate container and packaging locations and tidiness.	Materials, boxes, storage containers, and other items are stored in the appropriate place and orientated well for operations. Also, they are secure and not causing any danger to the workforce.		
	XI	Assess order and where items are found on the floor.	Nothing is sitting directly on the floor and no materials are left around the area. Items that need to be on the floor are clearly marked and positioned in designated areas clearly outlined on the floor.		
	XII	Easiness to access the tools for machines and measuring gauges.	Materials, tools, jigs, attachments, and fixtures are organized so that they are all easily within reach of the operator. Consider this as well for any kind of measuring tool or go/no-go devices.		
		Category Subtotal			
		Set in Order / Straighten Score: Subtotal divided by 6			
SHINE / SWEEP	XIII	The storage of gauges and tooling.	Arrangement of all fixtures, tools, and attachments are kept in clean area for storage and no risk of damage during transporting to storage.		
	XIV	Clear when equipment needs maintenance and when last maintained.	Buttons and switches on machinery marked, highlighted, and labeled. Check sheets clean and displayed. Maintenance is scheduled; levels of fluids, lubrication of joints are clearly itemized and illustrated.		
	XV	Assess the cleanliness of the work zone.	How dust free are the areas. Look under desks and behind work spaces to see if there is garbage and other unnecessary items.		
	XVI	Safety of the equipment, are areas gated off and safe for workers?	Spray shields and physical guards are in active use to keep items and liquids getting on the floor. Areas that are critical are clearly marked to protect workers.		
	XVII	Assess status of equipment in the area. Cleanliness overall appearance.	Are machines and equipment known to be on a schedule of cleaning?		
		Category Subtotal			
		Shine / Sweep Score: Subtotal divided by 5			
STANDARDIZE	XVIII	Is there visual color diagramming and color coding?	A clear and present color coding system is present in the work zone and across the company. It is clear that standards are being maintained and improved on.		
	XIX	Assess the access ways in case of emergency.	All emergency systems; fire vehicles, fire extinguishers, and emergency equipment free of obstruction and clear at all times. Access to electrical controls and fuses are known, marked, and free of any obstructions.		
	XX	The aisle ways are bright with light and clearly marked.	Walkways are clearly highlighted for direction, aisle access identified at any moment while in the work zone.		
	XXI	General area has quantity limits for materials and are marked clearly.	Heights are marked, quantity of materials are known, and min vs. max.		
	XXII	Is there clear document control of information in the work zone?	All information and documentation is controlled, labeled, and revisions are up to date. There are no label-less binders or pieces of paper in the area.		
		Category Subtotal			
		Standardize Score: Subtotal divided by 5			
SUSTAIN	XXIII	The aisle ways are clean and maintenance is clear.	Aisles are never full of anything and are clear for passage. All items and products not stored in the aisle and storage is next to aisle accessible for transportation.		
	XXIV	Illustrations and work zone plans are available to compare against.	5S has a maintenance system that allows for control of change and improvement of 5S in the work zones. Scoring is kept on each of these items and history is present and visible to support future improvement.		
	XXV	Ability for tools to be set back in place of storage.	No self-discipline is necessary to ensure that all tools, dies, jigs, and equipment are put back in the same spot. The effort of putting back should not require organizational skills.		
	XXVI	Evaluate the involvement of supervisors in 5S.	Supervisors are actively involved in the review process of 5S and are supporting improvement activities of the work areas.		
		Category Subtotal			
		Sustain Score: Subtotal divided by 4		**Total "Category Subtotals" divide by 26 average 5S score: TOTAL**	

5S Evaluation Review

Date: _____   Evaluation Area: _____

5S Element	Number	Evaluation Criteria	Rank these items from 1 through 5: 5 being well done	Score (1-5)	Ideas / Suggestions / Comments
SORT	I	Are the aisles and walkways open and clear?	All items that are not necessary or unsafe have been removed from the area where people travel and work.		
	II	Is the work zone free of any spills of fluids?	Consider whether there are any chemicals, lubricants, water, oils or other materials that may be hazardous in the area and on the floor.		
	III	Is the work zone free of unnecessary articles and items?	Are items that are not needed been removed from the work zone, i.e. tools, jigs, stationary, extra items.		
	IV	Is the work zone free of excess consumables/materials?	Evaluate against how many items are in the production work zone. Assess if the materials, parts, and supplies are currently needed for operations.		
	V	Is the information board active?	All announcements are displayed currently and in good presentable shape. Arrangement is straight and placed under appropriate headings.		
	VI	Are the areas walls and dividers free of items not used in operations?	Extra items are not on the walls, dividers, or hanging of signs that are not necessary.		
			Category Subtotal		
			Sort Score: Subtotal divided by 6		
SET IN ORDER / STRAIGHTEN	VII	Evaluate any documentation storage.	Only documents to do the job are stored at the work zone. These documents are stored nicely and in an orderly fashion that is recognizable to outsiders.		
	VIII	How are the shelves, desks, and work surfaces arranged?	All locations of items are labeled, marked, and it is known if they are missing.		
	IX	How are the tools and material used in operations stored?	No items are resting on walls or tucked in corners. No items are resting on equipment, cupboards, or other fixtures.		
	X	Evaluate container and packaging locations and tidiness.	Materials, boxes, storage containers, and other items are stored in the appropriate place and orientated well for operations. Also, they are secure and not causing any danger to the workforce.		
	XI	Assess order and where items are found on the floor.	Nothing is sitting directly on the floor and no materials are left around the area. Items that need to be on the floor are clearly marked and positioned in designated areas clearly outlined on the floor.		
	XII	Easiness to access the tools for machines and measuring gauges.	Materials, tools, jigs, attachments, and fixtures are organized so that they are all easily within reach of the operator. Consider this as well for any kind of measuring tool or go/no-go devices.		
			Category Subtotal		
			Set in Order / Straighten Score: Subtotal divided by 6		
SHINE / SWEEP	XIII	The storage of gauges and tooling.	Arrangement of all fixtures, tools, and attachments are kept in clean area for storage and no risk of damage during transporting to storage.		
	XIV	Clear when equipment needs maintenance and when last maintained.	Buttons and switches on machinery marked, highlighted, and labeled. Check sheets clean and displayed. Maintenance is scheduled; levels of fluids, lubrication of joints are clearly itemized and illustrated.		
	XV	Assess the cleanliness of the work zone.	How dust free are the areas. Look under desks and behind work spaces to see if there is garbage and other unnecessary items.		
	XVI	Safety of the equipment, are areas gated off and safe for workers?	Spray shields and physical guards are in active use to keep items and liquids getting on the floor. Areas that are critical are clearly marked to protect workers.		
	XVII	Assess status of equipment in the area. Cleanliness overall appearance.	Are machines and equipment known to be on a schedule of cleaning?		
			Category Subtotal		
			Shine / Sweep Score: Subtotal divided by 5		
STANDARDIZE	XVIII	Is there visual color diagramming and color coding?	A clear and present color coding system is present in the work zone and across the company. It is clear that standards are being maintained and improved on.		
	XIX	Assess the access ways in case of emergency.	All emergency systems; fire vehicles, fire extinguishers, and emergency equipment free of obstruction and clear at all times. Access to electrical controls and fuses are known, marked, and free of any obstructions.		
	XX	The aisle ways are bright with light and clearly marked.	Walkways are clearly highlighted for direction, aisle access identified at any moment while in the work zone.		
	XXI	General area has quantity limits for materials and are marked clearly.	Heights are marked, quantity of materials are known, and min vs. max.		
	XXII	Is there clear document control of information in the work zone?	All information and documentation is controlled, labeled, and revisions are up to date. There are no label-less binders or pieces of paper in the area.		
			Category Subtotal		
			Standardize Score: Subtotal divided by 5		
SUSTAIN	XXIII	The aisle ways are clean and maintenance is clear.	Aisles are never full of anything and are clear for passage. All items and products not stored in the aisle and storage is next to aisle accessible for transportation.		
	XXIV	Illustrations and work zone plans are available to compare against.	5S has a maintenance system that allows for control of change and improvement of 5S in the work zones. Scoring is kept on each of these items and history is present and visible to support future improvement.		
	XXV	Ability for tools to be set back in place of storage.	No self-discipline is necessary to ensure that all tools, dies, jigs, and equipment are put back in the same spot. The effort of putting back should not require organizational skills.		
	XXVI	Evaluate the involvement of supervisors in 5S.	Supervisors are actively involved in the review process of 5S and are supporting improvement activities of the work areas.		
			Category Subtotal		
			Sustain Score: Subtotal divided by 4		

 © **ENNA**™
KNOWLEDGE INTO PRACTICE

www.enna.com
www.productivitypress.com

Total "Category Subtotals" divide by 26 average 5S score: TOTAL

5S Evaluation Review

Date: _____   Evaluation Area:_____

5S Element	Number	Evaluation Criteria	Rank these items from 1 through 5: 5 being well done	Score (1-5)	Ideas / Suggestions / Comments
SORT	I	Are the aisles and walkways open and clear?	All items that are not necessary or unsafe have been removed from the area where people travel and work.		
	II	Is the work zone free of any spills of fluids?	Consider whether there are any chemicals, lubricants, water, oils or other materials that may be hazardous in the area and on the floor.		
	III	Is the work zone free of unnecessary articles and items?	Are items that are not needed been removed from the work zone, i.e. tools, jigs, stationary, extra items.		
	IV	Is the work zone free of excess consumables/materials?	Evaluate against how many items are in the production work zone. Assess if the materials, parts, and supplies are currently needed for operations.		
	V	Is the information board active?	All announcements are displayed currently and in good presentable shape. Arrangement is straight and placed under appropriate headings.		
	VI	Are the areas walls and dividers free of items not used in operations?	Extra items are not on the walls, dividers, or hanging of signs that are not necessary.		
		Category Subtotal			
		Sort Score: Subtotal divided by 6			
SET IN ORDER / STRAIGHTEN	VII	Evaluate any documentation storage.	Only documents to do the job are stored at the work zone. These documents are stored nicely and in an orderly fashion that is recognizable to outsiders.		
	VIII	How are the shelves, desks, and work surfaces arranged?	All locations of items are labeled, marked, and it is known if they are missing.		
	IX	How are the tools and material used in operations stored?	No items are resting on walls or tucked in corners. No items are resting on equipment, cupboards, or other fixtures.		
	X	Evaluate container and packaging locations and tidiness.	Materials, boxes, storage containers, and other items are stored in the appropriate place and orientated well for operations. Also, they are secure and not causing any danger to the workforce.		
	XI	Assess order and where items are found on the floor.	Nothing is sitting directly on the floor and no materials are left around the area. Items that need to be on the floor are clearly marked and positioned in designated areas clearly outlined on the floor.		
	XII	Easiness to access the tools for machines and measuring gauges.	Materials, tools, jigs, attachments, and fixtures are organized so that they are all easily within reach of the operator. Consider this as well for any kind of measuring tool or go/no-go devices.		
		Category Subtotal			
		Set in Order / Straighten Score: Subtotal divided by 6			
SHINE / SWEEP	XIII	The storage of gauges and tooling.	Arrangement of all fixtures, tools, and attachments are kept in clean area for storage and no risk of damage during transporting to storage.		
	XIV	Clear when equipment needs maintenance and when last maintained.	Buttons and switches on machinery marked, highlighted, and labeled. Check sheets clean and displayed. Maintenance is scheduled; levels of fluids, lubrication of joints are clearly itemized and illustrated.		
	XV	Assess the cleanliness of the work zone.	How dust free are the areas. Look under desks and behind work spaces to see if there is garbage and other unnecessary items.		
	XVI	Safety of the equipment, are areas gated off and safe for workers?	Spray shields and physical guards are in active use to keep items and liquids getting on the floor. Areas that are critical are clearly marked to protect workers.		
	XVII	Assess status of equipment in the area. Cleanliness overall appearance.	Are machines and equipment known to be on a schedule of cleaning?		
		Category Subtotal			
		Shine / Sweep Score: Subtotal divided by 5			
STANDARDIZE	XVIII	Is there visual color diagramming and color coding?	A clear and present color coding system is present in the work zone and across the company. It is clear that standards are being maintained and improved on.		
	XIX	Assess the access ways in case of emergency.	All emergency systems; fire vehicles, fire extinguishers, and emergency equipment free of obstruction and clear at all times. Access to electrical controls and fuses are known, marked, and free of any obstructions.		
	XX	The aisle ways are bright with light and clearly marked.	Walkways are clearly highlighted for direction, aisle access identified at any moment while in the work zone.		
	XXI	General area has quantity limits for materials and are marked clearly.	Heights are marked, quantity of materials are known, and min vs. max.		
	XXII	Is there clear document control of information in the work zone?	All information and documentation is controlled, labeled, and revisions are up to date. There are no label-less binders or pieces of paper in the area.		
		Category Subtotal			
		Standardize Score: Subtotal divided by 5			
SUSTAIN	XXIII	The aisle ways are clean and maintenance is clear.	Aisles are never full of anything and are clear for passage. All items and products not stored in the aisle and storage is next to aisle accessible for transportation.		
	XXIV	Illustrations and work zone plans are available to compare against.	5S has a maintenance system that allows for control of change and improvement of 5S in the work zones. Scoring is kept on each of these items and history is present and visible to support future improvement.		
	XXV	Ability for tools to be set back in place of storage.	No self-discipline is necessary to ensure that all tools, dies, jigs, and equipment are put back in the same spot. The effort of putting back should not require organizational skills.		
	XXVI	Evaluate the involvement of supervisors in 5S.	Supervisors are actively involved in the review process of 5S and are supporting improvement activities of the work areas.		
		Category Subtotal			
		Sustain Score: Subtotal divided by 4			

Total "Category Subtotals" divide by 26 average 5S score: TOTAL

5S Evaluation Review

Date: _____   Evaluation Area:_____

5S Element	Number	Evaluation Criteria	Rank these items from 1 through 5: 5 being well done	Score (1-5)	Ideas / Suggestions / Comments
SORT	I	Are the aisles and walkways open and clear?	All items that are not necessary or unsafe have been removed from the area where people travel and work.		
	II	Is the work zone free of any spills of fluids?	Consider whether there are any chemicals, lubricants, water, oils or other materials that may be hazardous in the area and on the floor.		
	III	Is the work zone free of unnecessary articles and items?	Are items that are not needed been removed from the work zone, i.e. tools, jigs, stationary, extra items.		
	IV	Is the work zone free of excess consumables/materials?	Evaluate against how many items are in the production work zone. Assess if the materials, parts, and supplies are currently needed for operations.		
	V	Is the information board active?	All announcements are displayed currently and in good presentable shape. Arrangement is straight and placed under appropriate headings.		
	VI	Are the areas walls and dividers free of items not used in operations?	Extra items are not on the walls, dividers, or hanging of signs that are not necessary.		
		Category Subtotal			
		Sort Score: Subtotal divided by 6			
SET IN ORDER / STRAIGHTEN	VII	Evaluate any documentation storage.	Only documents to do the job are stored at the work zone. These documents are stored nicely and in an orderly fashion that is recognizable to outsiders.		
	VIII	How are the shelves, desks, and work surfaces arranged?	All locations of items are labeled, marked, and it is known if they are missing.		
	IX	How are the tools and material used in operations stored?	No items are resting on walls or tucked in corners. No items are resting on equipment, cupboards, or other fixtures.		
	X	Evaluate container and packaging locations and tidiness.	Materials, boxes, storage containers, and other items are stored in the appropriate place and orientated well for operations. Also, they are secure and not causing any danger to the workforce.		
	XI	Assess order and where items are found on the floor.	Nothing is sitting directly on the floor and no materials are left around the area. Items that need to be on the floor are clearly marked and positioned in designated areas clearly outlined on the floor.		
	XII	Easiness to access the tools for machines and measuring gauges.	Materials, tools, jigs, attachments, and fixtures are organized so that they are all easily within reach of the operator. Consider this as well for any kind of measuring tool or go/no-go devices.		
		Category Subtotal			
		Set in Order / Straighten Score: Subtotal divided by 6			
SHINE / SWEEP	XIII	The storage of gauges and tooling.	Arrangement of all fixtures, tools, and attachments are kept in clean area for storage and no risk of damage during transporting to storage.		
	XIV	Clear when equipment needs maintenance and when last maintained.	Buttons and switches on machinery marked, highlighted, and labeled. Check sheets clean and displayed. Maintenance is scheduled; levels of fluids, lubrication of joints are clearly itemized and illustrated.		
	XV	Assess the cleanliness of the work zone.	How dust free are the areas. Look under desks and behind work spaces to see if there is garbage and other unnecessary items.		
	XVI	Safety of the equipment, are areas gated off and safe for workers?	Spray shields and physical guards are in active use to keep items and liquids getting on the floor. Areas that are critical are clearly marked to protect workers.		
	XVII	Assess status of equipment in the area. Cleanliness overall appearance.	Are machines and equipment known to be on a schedule of cleaning?		
		Category Subtotal			
		Shine / Sweep Score: Subtotal divided by 5			
STANDARDIZE	XVIII	Is there visual color diagramming and color coding?	A clear and present color coding system is present in the work zone and across the company. It is clear that standards are being maintained and improved on.		
	XIX	Assess the access ways in case of emergency.	All emergency systems; fire vehicles, fire extinguishers, and emergency equipment free of obstruction and clear at all times. Access to electrical controls and fuses are known, marked, and free of any obstructions.		
	XX	The aisle ways are bright with light and clearly marked.	Walkways are clearly highlighted for direction, aisle access identified at any moment while in the work zone.		
	XXI	General area has quantity limits for materials and are marked clearly.	Heights are marked, quantity of materials are known, and min vs. max.		
	XXII	Is there clear document control of information in the work zone?	All information and documentation is controlled, labeled, and revisions are up to date. There are no label-less binders or pieces of paper in the area.		
		Category Subtotal			
		Standardize Score: Subtotal divided by 5			
SUSTAIN	XXIII	The aisle ways are clean and maintenance is clear.	Aisles are never full of anything and are clear for passage. All items and products not stored in the aisle and storage is next to aisle accessible for transportation.		
	XXIV	Illustrations and work zone plans are available to compare against.	5S has a maintenance system that allows for control of change and improvement of 5S in the work zones. Scoring is kept on each of these items and history is present and visible to support future improvement.		
	XXV	Ability for tools to be set back in place of storage.	No self-discipline is necessary to ensure that all tools, dies, jigs, and equipment are put back in the same spot. The effort of putting back should not require organizational skills.		
	XXVI	Evaluate the involvement of supervisors in 5S.	Supervisors are actively involved in the review process of 5S and are supporting improvement activities of the work areas.		
		Category Subtotal			
		Sustain Score: Subtotal divided by 4			

Total "Category Subtotals" divide by 26 average 5S score: TOTAL

5S Evaluation Review

Date: _____   Evaluation Area: _____

5S Element	Number	Evaluation Criteria	Rank these items from 1 through 5: 5 being well done	Score (1-5)	Ideas / Suggestions / Comments
SORT	I	Are the aisles and walkways open and clear?	All items that are not necessary or unsafe have been removed from the area where people travel and work.		
	II	Is the work zone free of any spills of fluids?	Consider whether there are any chemicals, lubricants, water, oils or other materials that may be hazardous in the area and on the floor.		
	III	Is the work zone free of unnecessary articles and items?	Are items that are not needed been removed from the work zone, i.e. tools, jigs, stationary, extra items.		
	IV	Is the work zone free of excess consumables/materials?	Evaluate against how many items are in the production work zone. Assess if the materials, parts, and supplies are currently needed for operations.		
	V	Is the information board active?	All announcements are displayed currently and in good presentable shape. Arrangement is straight and placed under appropriate headings.		
	VI	Are the areas walls and dividers free of items not used in operations?	Extra items are not on the walls, dividers, or hanging of signs that are not necessary.		
			Category Subtotal		
			Sort Score: Subtotal divided by 6		
SET IN ORDER / STRAIGHTEN	VII	Evaluate any documentation storage.	Only documents to do the job are stored at the work zone. These documents are stored nicely and in an orderly fashion that is recognizable to outsiders.		
	VIII	How are the shelves, desks, and work surfaces arranged?	All locations of items are labeled, marked, and it is known if they are missing.		
	IX	How are the tools and material used in operations stored?	No items are resting on walls or tucked in corners. No items are resting on equipment, cupboards, or other fixtures.		
	X	Evaluate container and packaging locations and tidiness.	Materials, boxes, storage containers, and other items are stored in the appropriate place and orientated well for operations. Also, they are secure and not causing any danger to the workforce.		
	XI	Assess order and where items are found on the floor.	Nothing is sitting directly on the floor and no materials are left around the area. Items that need to be on the floor are clearly marked and positioned in designated areas clearly outlined on the floor.		
	XII	Easiness to access the tools for machines and measuring gauges.	Materials, tools, jigs, attachments, and fixtures are organized so that they are all easily within reach of the operator. Consider this as well for any kind of measuring tool or go/no-go devices.		
			Category Subtotal		
			Set in Order / Straighten Score: Subtotal divided by 6		
SHINE / SWEEP	XIII	The storage of gauges and tooling.	Arrangement of all fixtures, tools, and attachments are kept in clean area for storage and no risk of damage during transporting to storage.		
	XIV	Clear when equipment needs maintenance and when last maintained.	Buttons and switches on machinery marked, highlighted, and labeled. Check sheets clean and displayed. Maintenance is scheduled; levels of fluids, lubrication of joints are clearly itemized and illustrated.		
	XV	Assess the cleanliness of the work zone.	How dust free are the areas. Look under desks and behind work spaces to see if there is garbage and other unnecessary items.		
	XVI	Safety of the equipment, are areas gated off and safe for workers?	Spray shields and physical guards are in active use to keep items and liquids getting on the floor. Areas that are critical are clearly marked to protect workers.		
	XVII	Assess status of equipment in the area. Cleanliness overall appearance.	Are machines and equipment known to be on a schedule of cleaning?		
			Category Subtotal		
			Shine / Sweep Score: Subtotal divided by 5		
STANDARDIZE	XVIII	Is there visual color diagramming and color coding?	A clear and present color coding system is present in the work zone and across the company. It is clear that standards are being maintained and improved on.		
	XIX	Assess the access ways in case of emergency.	All emergency systems; fire vehicles, fire extinguishers, and emergency equipment free of obstruction and clear at all times. Access to electrical controls and fuses are known, marked, and free of any obstructions.		
	XX	The aisle ways are bright with light and clearly marked.	Walkways are clearly highlighted for direction, aisle access identified at any moment while in the work zone.		
	XXI	General area has quantity limits for materials and are marked clearly.	Heights are marked, quantity of materials are known, and min vs. max.		
	XXII	Is there clear document control of information in the work zone?	All information and documentation is controlled, labeled, and revisions are up to date. There are no label-less binders or pieces of paper in the area.		
			Category Subtotal		
			Standardize Score: Subtotal divided by 5		
SUSTAIN	XXIII	The aisle ways are clean and maintenance is clear.	Aisles are never full of anything and are clear for passage. All items and products not stored in the aisle and storage is next to aisle accessible for transportation.		
	XXIV	Illustrations and work zone plans are available to compare against.	5S has a maintenance system that allows for control of change and improvement of 5S in the work zones. Scoring is kept on each of these items and history is present and visible to support future improvement.		
	XXV	Ability for tools to be set back in place of storage.	No self-discipline is necessary to ensure that all tools, dies, jigs, and equipment are put back in the same spot. The effort of putting back should not require organizational skills.		
	XXVI	Evaluate the involvement of supervisors in 5S.	Supervisors are actively involved in the review process of 5S and are supporting improvement activities of the work areas.		
			Category Subtotal		
			Sustain Score: Subtotal divided by 4		**Total "Category Subtotals" divide by 26 average 5S score: TOTAL**

5S Evaluation Review

Date: _____   Evaluation Area: _____

5S Element	Number	Evaluation Criteria	Rank these items from 1 through 5: 5 being well done	Score (1-5)	Ideas / Suggestions / Comments
SORT	I	Are the aisles and walkways open and clear?	All items that are not necessary or unsafe have been removed from the area where people travel and work.		
	II	Is the work zone free of any spills of fluids?	Consider whether there are any chemicals, lubricants, water, oils or other materials that may be hazardous in the area and on the floor.		
	III	Is the work zone free of unnecessary articles and items?	Are items that are not needed been removed from the work zone, i.e. tools, jigs, stationary, extra items.		
	IV	Is the work zone free of excess consumables/materials?	Evaluate against how many items are in the production work zone. Assess if the materials, parts, and supplies are currently needed for operations.		
	V	Is the information board active?	All announcements are displayed currently and in good presentable shape. Arrangement is straight and placed under appropriate headings.		
	VI	Are the areas walls and dividers free of items not used in operations?	Extra items are not on the walls, dividers, or hanging of signs that are not necessary.		
			Category Subtotal		
			Sort Score: Subtotal divided by 6		
SET IN ORDER / STRAIGHTEN	VII	Evaluate any documentation storage.	Only documents to do the job are stored at the work zone. These documents are stored nicely and in an orderly fashion that is recognizable to outsiders.		
	VIII	How are the shelves, desks, and work surfaces arranged?	All locations of items are labeled, marked, and it is known if they are missing.		
	IX	How are the tools and material used in operations stored?	No items are resting on walls or tucked in corners. No items are resting on equipment, cupboards, or other fixtures.		
	X	Evaluate container and packaging locations and tidiness.	Materials, boxes, storage containers, and other items are stored in the appropriate place and orientated well for operations. Also, they are secure and not causing any danger to the workforce.		
	XI	Assess order and where items are found on the floor.	Nothing is sitting directly on the floor and no materials are left around the area. Items that need to be on the floor are clearly marked and positioned in designated areas clearly outlined on the floor.		
	XII	Easiness to access the tools for machines and measuring gauges.	Materials, tools, jigs, attachments, and fixtures are organized so that they are all easily within reach of the operator. Consider this as well for any kind of measuring tool or go/no-go devices.		
			Category Subtotal		
			Set in Order / Straighten Score: Subtotal divided by 6		
SHINE / SWEEP	XIII	The storage of gauges and tooling.	Arrangement of all fixtures, tools, and attachments are kept in clean area for storage and no risk of damage during transporting to storage.		
	XIV	Clear when equipment needs maintenance and when last maintained.	Buttons and switches on machinery marked, highlighted, and labeled. Check sheets clean and displayed. Maintenance is scheduled; levels of fluids, lubrication of joints are clearly itemized and illustrated.		
	XV	Assess the cleanliness of the work zone.	How dust free are the areas. Look under desks and behind work spaces to see if there is garbage and other unnecessary items.		
	XVI	Safety of the equipment, are areas gated off and safe for workers?	Spray shields and physical guards are in active use to keep items and liquids getting on the floor. Areas that are critical are clearly marked to protect workers.		
	XVII	Assess status of equipment in the area. Cleanliness overall appearance.	Are machines and equipment known to be on a schedule of cleaning?		
			Category Subtotal		
			Shine / Sweep Score: Subtotal divided by 5		
STANDARDIZE	XVIII	Is there visual color diagramming and color coding?	A clear and present color coding system is present in the work zone and across the company. It is clear that standards are being maintained and improved on.		
	XIX	Assess the access ways in case of emergency.	All emergency systems; fire vehicles, fire extinguishers, and emergency equipment free of obstruction and clear at all times. Access to electrical controls and fuses are known, marked, and free of any obstructions.		
	XX	The aisle ways are bright with light and clearly marked.	Walkways are clearly highlighted for direction, aisle access identified at any moment while in the work zone.		
	XXI	General area has quantity limits for materials and are marked clearly.	Heights are marked, quantity of materials are known, and min vs. max.		
	XXII	Is there clear document control of information in the work zone?	All information and documentation is controlled, labeled, and revisions are up to date. There are no label-less binders or pieces of paper in the area.		
			Category Subtotal		
			Standardize Score: Subtotal divided by 5		
SUSTAIN	XXIII	The aisle ways are clean and maintenance is clear.	Aisles are never full of anything and are clear for passage. All items and products not stored in the aisle and storage is next to aisle accessible for transportation.		
	XXIV	Illustrations and work zone plans are available to compare against.	5S has a maintenance system that allows for control of change and improvement of 5S in the work zones. Scoring is kept on each of these items and history is present and visible to support future improvement.		
	XXV	Ability for tools to be set back in place of storage.	No self-discipline is necessary to ensure that all tools, dies, jigs, and equipment are put back in the same spot. The effort of putting back should not require organizational skills.		
	XXVI	Evaluate the involvement of supervisors in 5S.	Supervisors are actively involved in the review process of 5S and are supporting improvement activities of the work areas.		
			Category Subtotal		
			Sustain Score: Subtotal divided by 4		**Total "Category Subtotals" divide by 26 average 5S score: TOTAL**

5S Evaluation Review

Date: _____   Evaluation Area: _____

5S Element	Number	Evaluation Criteria	Rank these items from 1 through 5: 5 being well done	Score (1-5)	Ideas / Suggestions / Comments
SORT	I	Are the aisles and walkways open and clear?	All items that are not necessary or unsafe have been removed from the area where people travel and work.		
	II	Is the work zone free of any spills of fluids?	Consider whether there are any chemicals, lubricants, water, oils or other materials that may be hazardous in the area and on the floor.		
	III	Is the work zone free of unnecessary articles and items?	Are items that are not needed been removed from the work zone, i.e. tools, jigs, stationary, extra items.		
	IV	Is the work zone free of excess consumables/materials?	Evaluate against how many items are in the production work zone. Assess if the materials, parts, and supplies are currently needed for operations.		
	V	Is the information board active?	All announcements are displayed currently and in good presentable shape. Arrangement is straight and placed under appropriate headings.		
	VI	Are the areas walls and dividers free of items not used in operations?	Extra items are not on the walls, dividers, or hanging of signs that are not necessary.		
			Category Subtotal		
			Sort Score: Subtotal divided by 6		
SET IN ORDER / STRAIGHTEN	VII	Evaluate any documentation storage.	Only documents to do the job are stored at the work zone. These documents are stored nicely and in an orderly fashion that is recognizable to outsiders.		
	VIII	How are the shelves, desks, and work surfaces arranged?	All locations of items are labeled, marked, and it is known if they are missing.		
	IX	How are the tools and material used in operations stored?	No items are resting on walls or tucked in corners. No items are resting on equipment, cupboards, or other fixtures.		
	X	Evaluate container and packaging locations and tidiness.	Materials, boxes, storage containers, and other items are stored in the appropriate place and orientated well for operations. Also, they are secure and not causing any danger to the workforce.		
	XI	Assess order and where items are found on the floor.	Nothing is sitting directly on the floor and no materials are left around the area. Items that need to be on the floor are clearly marked and positioned in designated areas clearly outlined on the floor.		
	XII	Easiness to access the tools for machines and measuring gauges.	Materials, tools, jigs, attachments, and fixtures are organized so that they are all easily within reach of the operator. Consider this as well for any kind of measuring tool or go/no-go devices.		
			Category Subtotal		
			Set in Order / Straighten Score: Subtotal divided by 6		
SHINE / SWEEP	XIII	The storage of gauges and tooling.	Arrangement of all fixtures, tools, and attachments are kept in clean area for storage and no risk of damage during transporting to storage.		
	XIV	Clear when equipment needs maintenance and when last maintained.	Buttons and switches on machinery marked, highlighted, and labeled. Check sheets clean and displayed. Maintenance is scheduled; levels of fluids, lubrication of joints are clearly itemized and illustrated.		
	XV	Assess the cleanliness of the work zone.	How dust free are the areas. Look under desks and behind work spaces to see if there is garbage and other unnecessary items.		
	XVI	Safety of the equipment, are areas gated off and safe for workers?	Spray shields and physical guards are in active use to keep items and liquids getting on the floor. Areas that are critical are clearly marked to protect workers.		
	XVII	Assess status of equipment in the area. Cleanliness overall appearance.	Are machines and equipment known to be on a schedule of cleaning?		
			Category Subtotal		
			Shine / Sweep Score: Subtotal divided by 5		
STANDARDIZE	XVIII	Is there visual color diagramming and color coding?	A clear and present color coding system is present in the work zone and across the company. It is clear that standards are being maintained and improved on.		
	XIX	Assess the access ways in case of emergency.	All emergency systems; fire vehicles, fire extinguishers, and emergency equipment free of obstruction and clear at all times. Access to electrical controls and fuses are known, marked, and free of any obstructions.		
	XX	The aisle ways are bright with light and clearly marked.	Walkways are clearly highlighted for direction, aisle access identified at any moment while in the work zone.		
	XXI	General area has quantity limits for materials and are marked clearly.	Heights are marked, quantity of materials are known, and min vs. max.		
	XXII	Is there clear document control of information in the work zone?	All information and documentation is controlled, labeled, and revisions are up to date. There are no label-less binders or pieces of paper in the area.		
			Category Subtotal		
			Standardize Score: Subtotal divided by 5		
SUSTAIN	XXIII	The aisle ways are clean and maintenance is clear.	Aisles are never full of anything and are clear for passage. All items and products not stored in the aisle and storage is next to aisle accessible for transportation.		
	XXIV	Illustrations and work zone plans are available to compare against.	5S has a maintenance system that allows for control of change and improvement of 5S in the work zones. Scoring is kept on each of these areas and history is present and visible to support future improvement.		
	XXV	Ability for tools to be set back in place of storage.	No self-discipline is necessary to ensure that all tools, dies, jigs, and equipment are put back in the same spot. The effort of putting back should not require organizational skills.		
	XXVI	Evaluate the involvement of supervisors in 5S.	Supervisors are actively involved in the review process of 5S and are supporting improvement activities of the work areas.		
			Category Subtotal		
			Sustain Score: Subtotal divided by 4		

Total "Category Subtotals" divide by 26 average 5S score: TOTAL

5S Evaluation Review

Date: _____   Evaluation Area: _____

5S Element	Number	Evaluation Criteria	Rank these items from 1 through 5: 5 being well done	Score (1-5)	Ideas / Suggestions / Comments
SORT	I	Are the aisles and walkways open and clear?	All items that are not necessary or unsafe have been removed from the area where people travel and work.		
	II	Is the work zone free of any spills of fluids?	Consider whether there are any chemicals, lubricants, water, oils or other materials that may be hazardous in the area and on the floor.		
	III	Is the work zone free of unnecessary articles and items?	Are items that are not needed been removed from the work zone, i.e. tools, jigs, stationary, extra items.		
	IV	Is the work zone free of excess consumables/materials?	Evaluate against how many items are in the production work zone. Assess if the materials, parts, and supplies are currently needed for operations.		
	V	Is the information board active?	All announcements are displayed currently and in good presentable shape. Arrangement is straight and placed under appropriate headings.		
	VI	Are the areas walls and dividers free of items not used in operations?	Extra items are not on the walls, dividers, or hanging of signs that are not necessary.		
		Category Subtotal			
		Sort Score: Subtotal divided by 6			
SET IN ORDER / STRAIGHTEN	VII	Evaluate any documentation storage.	Only documents to do the job are stored at the work zone. These documents are stored nicely and in an orderly fashion that is recognizable to outsiders.		
	VIII	How are the shelves, desks, and work surfaces arranged?	All locations of items are labeled, marked, and it is known if they are missing.		
	IX	How are the tools and material used in operations stored?	No items are resting on walls or tucked in corners. No items are resting on equipment, cupboards, or other fixtures.		
	X	Evaluate container and packaging locations and tidiness.	Materials, boxes, storage containers, and other items are stored in the appropriate place and orientated well for operations. Also, they are secure and not causing any danger to the workforce.		
	XI	Assess order and where items are found on the floor.	Nothing is sitting directly on the floor and no materials are left around the area. Items that need to be on the floor are clearly marked and positioned in designated areas clearly outlined on the floor.		
	XII	Easiness to access the tools for machines and measuring gauges.	Materials, tools, jigs, attachments, and fixtures are organized so that they are all easily within reach of the operator. Consider this as well for any kind of measuring tool or go/no-go devices.		
		Category Subtotal			
		Set in Order / Straighten Score: Subtotal divided by 6			
SHINE / SWEEP	XIII	The storage of gauges and tooling.	Arrangement of all fixtures, tools, and attachments are kept in clean area for storage and no risk of damage during transporting to storage.		
	XIV	Clear when equipment needs maintenance and when last maintained.	Buttons and switches on machinery marked, highlighted, and labeled. Check sheets clean and displayed. Maintenance is scheduled; levels of fluids, lubrication of joints are clearly itemized and illustrated.		
	XV	Assess the cleanliness of the work zone.	How dust free are the areas. Look under desks and behind work spaces to see if there is garbage and other unnecessary items.		
	XVI	Safety of the equipment, are areas gated off and safe for workers?	Spray shields and physical guards are in active use to keep items and liquids getting on the floor. Areas that are critical are clearly marked to protect workers.		
	XVII	Assess status of equipment in the area. Cleanliness overall appearance.	Are machines and equipment known to be on a schedule of cleaning?		
		Category Subtotal			
		Shine / Sweep Score: Subtotal divided by 5			
STANDARDIZE	XVIII	Is there visual color diagramming and color coding?	A clear and present color coding system is present in the work zone and across the company. It is clear that standards are being maintained and improved on.		
	XIX	Assess the access ways in case of emergency.	All emergency systems; fire vehicles, fire extinguishers, and emergency equipment free of obstruction and clear at all times. Access to electrical controls and fuses are known, marked, and free of any obstructions.		
	XX	The aisle ways are bright with light and clearly marked.	Walkways are clearly highlighted for direction, aisle access identified at any moment while in the work zone.		
	XXI	General area has quantity limits for materials and are marked clearly.	Heights are marked, quantity of materials are known, and min vs. max.		
	XXII	Is there clear document control of information in the work zone?	All information and documentation is controlled, labeled, and revisions are up to date. There are no label-less binders or pieces of paper in the area.		
		Category Subtotal			
		Standardize Score: Subtotal divided by 5			
SUSTAIN	XXIII	The aisle ways are clean and maintenance is clear.	Aisles are never full of anything and are clear for passage. All items and products not stored in the aisle and storage is next to aisle accessible for transportation.		
	XXIV	Illustrations and work zone plans are available to compare against.	5S has a maintenance system that allows for control of change and improvement of 5S in the work zones. Scoring is kept on each of these items and history is present and visible to support future improvement.		
	XXV	Ability for tools to be set back in place of storage.	No self-discipline is necessary to ensure that all tools, dies, jigs, and equipment are put back in the same spot. The effort of putting back should not require organizational skills.		
	XXVI	Evaluate the involvement of supervisors in 5S.	Supervisors are actively involved in the review process of 5S and are supporting improvement activities of the work areas.		
		Category Subtotal			
		Sustain Score: Subtotal divided by 4			

Total "Category Subtotals" divide by 26 average 5S score: TOTAL

5S Evaluation Review

Date: _____   Evaluation Area: _____

5S Element	Number	Evaluation Criteria	Rank these items from 1 through 5: 5 being well done	Score (1-5)	Ideas / Suggestions / Comments
SORT	I	Are the aisles and walkways open and clear?	All items that are not necessary or unsafe have been removed from the area where people travel and work.		
	II	Is the work zone free of any spills of fluids?	Consider whether there are any chemicals, lubricants, water, oils or other materials that may be hazardous in the area and on the floor.		
	III	Is the work zone free of unnecessary articles and items?	Are items that are not needed been removed from the work zone, i.e. tools, jigs, stationary, extra items.		
	IV	Is the work zone free of excess consumables/materials?	Evaluate against how many items are in the production work zone. Assess if the materials, parts, and supplies are currently needed for operations.		
	V	Is the information board active?	All announcements are displayed currently and in good presentable shape. Arrangement is straight and placed under appropriate headings.		
	VI	Are the areas walls and dividers free of items not used in operations?	Extra items are not on the walls, dividers, or hanging of signs that are not necessary.		
			Category Subtotal		
			Sort Score: Subtotal divided by 6		
SET IN ORDER / STRAIGHTEN	VII	Evaluate any documentation storage.	Only documents to do the job are stored at the work zone. These documents are stored nicely and in an orderly fashion that is recognizable to outsiders.		
	VIII	How are the shelves, desks, and work surfaces arranged?	All locations of items are labeled, marked, and it is known if they are missing.		
	IX	How are the tools and material used in operations stored?	No items are resting on walls or tucked in corners. No items are resting on equipment, cupboards, or other fixtures.		
	X	Evaluate container and packaging locations and tidiness.	Materials, boxes, storage containers, and other items are stored in the appropriate place and orientated well for operations. Also, they are secure and not causing any danger to the workforce.		
	XI	Assess order and where items are found on the floor.	Nothing is sitting directly on the floor and no materials are left around the area. Items that need to be on the floor are clearly marked and positioned in designated areas clearly outlined on the floor.		
	XII	Easiness to access the tools for machines and measuring gauges.	Materials, tools, jigs, attachments, and fixtures are organized so that they are all easily within reach of the operator. Consider this as well for any kind of measuring tool or go/no-go devices.		
			Category Subtotal		
			Set in Order / Straighten Score: Subtotal divided by 6		
SHINE / SWEEP	XIII	The storage of gauges and tooling.	Arrangement of all fixtures, tools, and attachments are kept in clean area for storage and no risk of damage during transporting to storage.		
	XIV	Clear when equipment needs maintenance and when last maintained.	Buttons and switches on machinery marked, highlighted, and labeled. Check sheets clean and displayed. Maintenance is scheduled; levels of fluids, lubrication of joints are clearly itemized and illustrated.		
	XV	Assess the cleanliness of the work zone.	How dust free are the areas. Look under desks and behind work spaces to see if there is garbage and other unnecessary items.		
	XVI	Safety of the equipment, are areas gated off and safe for workers?	Spray shields and physical guards are in active use to keep items and liquids getting on the floor. Areas that are critical are clearly marked to protect workers.		
	XVII	Assess status of equipment in the area. Cleanliness overall appearance.	Are machines and equipment known to be on a schedule of cleaning?		
			Category Subtotal		
			Shine / Sweep Score: Subtotal divided by 5		
STANDARDIZE	XVIII	Is there visual color diagramming and color coding?	A clear and present color coding system is present in the work zone and across the company. It is clear that standards are being maintained and improved on.		
	XIX	Assess the access ways in case of emergency.	All emergency systems; fire vehicles, fire extinguishers, and emergency equipment free of obstruction and clear at all times. Access to electrical controls and fuses are known, marked, and free of any obstructions.		
	XX	The aisle ways are bright with light and clearly marked.	Walkways are clearly highlighted for direction, aisle access identified at any moment while in the work zone.		
	XXI	General area has quantity limits for materials and are marked clearly.	Heights are marked, quantity of materials are known, and min vs. max.		
	XXII	Is there clear document control of information in the work zone?	All information and documentation is controlled, labeled, and revisions are up to date. There are no label-less binders or pieces of paper in the area.		
			Category Subtotal		
			Standardize Score: Subtotal divided by 5		
SUSTAIN	XXIII	The aisle ways are clean and maintenance is clear.	Aisles are never full of anything and are clear for passage. All items and products not stored in the aisle and storage is next to aisle accessible for transportation.		
	XXIV	Illustrations and work zone plans are available to compare against.	5S has a maintenance system that allows for control of change and improvement of 5S in the work zones. Scoring is kept on each of these items and history is present and visible to support future improvement.		
	XXV	Ability for tools to be set back in place of storage.	No self-discipline is necessary to ensure that all tools, dies, jigs, and equipment are put back in the same spot. The effort of putting back should not require organizational skills.		
	XXVI	Evaluate the involvement of supervisors in 5S.	Supervisors are actively involved in the review process of 5S and are supporting improvement activities of the work areas.		
			Category Subtotal		
			Sustain Score: Subtotal divided by 4		

Total "Category Subtotals" divide by 26 average 5S score: TOTAL

5S Evaluation Review

Date: _____   Evaluation Area: _____

5S Element	Number	Evaluation Criteria	Rank these items from 1 through 5: 5 being well done	Score (1-5)	Ideas / Suggestions / Comments
SORT	I	Are the aisles and walkways open and clear?	All items that are not necessary or unsafe have been removed from the area where people travel and work.		
	II	Is the work zone free of any spills of fluids?	Consider whether there are any chemicals, lubricants, water, oils or other materials that may be hazardous in the area and on the floor.		
	III	Is the work zone free of unnecessary articles and items?	Are items that are not needed been removed from the work zone, i.e. tools, jigs, stationary, extra items.		
	IV	Is the work zone free of excess consumables/materials?	Evaluate against how many items are in the production work zone. Assess if the materials, parts, and supplies are currently needed for operations.		
	V	Is the information board active?	All announcements are displayed currently and in good presentable shape. Arrangement is straight and placed under appropriate headings.		
	VI	Are the areas walls and dividers free of items not used in operations?	Extra items are not on the walls, dividers, or hanging of signs that are not necessary.		
			Category Subtotal		
			Sort Score: Subtotal divided by 6		
SET IN ORDER / STRAIGHTEN	VII	Evaluate any documentation storage.	Only documents to do the job are stored at the work zone. These documents are stored nicely and in an orderly fashion that is recognizable to outsiders.		
	VIII	How are the shelves, desks, and work surfaces arranged?	All locations of items are labeled, marked, and it is known if they are missing.		
	IX	How are the tools and material used in operations stored?	No items are resting on walls or tucked in corners. No items are resting on equipment, cupboards, or other fixtures.		
	X	Evaluate container and packaging locations and tidiness.	Materials, boxes, storage containers, and other items are stored in the appropriate place and orientated well for operations. Also, they are secure and not causing any danger to the workforce.		
	XI	Assess order and where items are found on the floor.	Nothing is sitting directly on the floor and no materials are left around the area. Items that need to be on the floor are clearly marked and positioned in designated areas clearly outlined on the floor.		
	XII	Easiness to access the tools for machines and measuring gauges.	Materials, tools, jigs, attachments, and fixtures are organized so that they are all easily within reach of the operator. Consider this as well for any kind of measuring tool or go/no-go devices.		
			Category Subtotal		
			Set in Order / Straighten Score: Subtotal divided by 6		
SHINE / SWEEP	XIII	The storage of gauges and tooling.	Arrangement of all fixtures, tools, and attachments are kept in clean area for storage and no risk of damage during transporting to storage.		
	XIV	Clear when equipment needs maintenance and when last maintained.	Buttons and switches on machinery marked, highlighted, and labeled. Check sheets clean and displayed. Maintenance is scheduled; levels of fluids, lubrication of joints are clearly itemized and illustrated.		
	XV	Assess the cleanliness of the work zone.	How dust free are the areas. Look under desks and behind work spaces to see if there is garbage and other unnecessary items.		
	XVI	Safety of the equipment, are areas gated off and safe for workers?	Spray shields and physical guards are in active use to keep items and liquids getting on the floor. Areas that are critical are clearly marked to protect workers.		
	XVII	Assess status of equipment in the area. Cleanliness overall appearance.	Are machines and equipment known to be on a schedule of cleaning?		
			Category Subtotal		
			Shine / Sweep Score: Subtotal divided by 5		
STANDARDIZE	XVIII	Is there visual color diagramming and color coding?	A clear and present color coding system is present in the work zone and across the company. It is clear that standards are being maintained and improved on.		
	XIX	Assess the access ways in case of emergency.	All emergency systems; fire vehicles, fire extinguishers, and emergency equipment free of obstruction and clear at all times. Access to electrical controls and fuses are known, marked, and free of any obstructions.		
	XX	The aisle ways are bright with light and clearly marked.	Walkways are clearly highlighted for direction, aisle access identified at any moment while in the work zone.		
	XXI	General area has quantity limits for materials and are marked clearly.	Heights are marked, quantity of materials are known, and min vs. max.		
	XXII	Is there clear document control of information in the work zone?	All information and documentation is controlled, labeled, and revisions are up to date. There are no label-less binders or pieces of paper in the area.		
			Category Subtotal		
			Standardize Score: Subtotal divided by 5		
SUSTAIN	XXIII	The aisle ways are clean and maintenance is clear.	Aisles are never full of anything and are clear for passage. All items and products not stored in the aisle and storage is next to aisle accessible for transportation.		
	XXIV	Illustrations and work zone plans are available to compare against.	5S has a maintenance system that allows for control of change and improvement of 5S in the work zones. Scoring is kept on each of these items and history is present and visible to support future improvement.		
	XXV	Ability for tools to be set back in place of storage.	No self-discipline is necessary to ensure that all tools, dies, jigs, and equipment are put back in the same spot. The effort of putting back should not require organizational skills.		
	XXVI	Evaluate the involvement of supervisors in 5S.	Supervisors are actively involved in the review process of 5S and are supporting improvement activities of the work areas.		
			Category Subtotal		
			Sustain Score: Subtotal divided by 4		**Total "Category Subtotals" divide by 26 average 5S score: TOTAL**

5S Evaluation Review

Date: _____   Evaluation Area: _____

5S Element	Number	Evaluation Criteria	Rank these items from 1 through 5: 5 being well done	Score (1-5)	Ideas / Suggestions / Comments
SORT	I	Are the aisles and walkways open and clear?	All items that are not necessary or unsafe have been removed from the area where people travel and work.		
	II	Is the work zone free of any spills of fluids?	Consider whether there are any chemicals, lubricants, water, oils or other materials that may be hazardous in the area and on the floor.		
	III	Is the work zone free of unnecessary articles and items?	Are items that are not needed been removed from the work zone, i.e. tools, jigs, stationary, extra items.		
	IV	Is the work zone free of excess consumables/materials?	Evaluate against how many items are in the production work zone. Assess if the materials, parts, and supplies are currently needed for operations.		
	V	Is the information board active?	All announcements are displayed currently and in good presentable shape. Arrangement is straight and placed under appropriate headings.		
	VI	Are the areas walls and dividers free of items not used in operations?	Extra items are not on the walls, dividers, or hanging of signs that are not necessary.		
			Category Subtotal		
			Sort Score: Subtotal divided by 6		
SET IN ORDER / STRAIGHTEN	VII	Evaluate any documentation storage.	Only documents to do the job are stored at the work zone. These documents are stored nicely and in an orderly fashion that is recognizable to outsiders.		
	VIII	How are the shelves, desks, and work surfaces arranged?	All locations of items are labeled, marked, and it is known if they are missing.		
	IX	How are the tools and material used in operations stored?	No items are resting on walls or tucked in corners. No items are resting on equipment, cupboards, or other fixtures.		
	X	Evaluate container and packaging locations and tidiness.	Materials, boxes, storage containers, and other items are stored in the appropriate place and orientated well for operations. Also, they are secure and not causing any danger to the workforce.		
	XI	Assess order and where items are found on the floor.	Nothing is sitting directly on the floor and no materials are left around the area. Items that need to be on the floor are clearly marked and positioned in designated areas clearly outlined on the floor.		
	XII	Easiness to access the tools for machines and measuring gauges.	Materials, tools, jigs, attachments, and fixtures are organized so that they are all easily within reach of the operator. Consider this as well for any kind of measuring tool or go/no-go devices.		
			Category Subtotal		
			Set in Order / Straighten Score: Subtotal divided by 6		
SHINE / SWEEP	XIII	The storage of gauges and tooling.	Arrangement of all fixtures, tools, and attachments are kept in clean area for storage and no risk of damage during transporting to storage.		
	XIV	Clear when equipment needs maintenance and when last maintained.	Buttons and switches on machinery marked, highlighted, and labeled. Check sheets clean and displayed. Maintenance is scheduled; levels of fluids, lubrication of joints are clearly itemized and illustrated.		
	XV	Assess the cleanliness of the work zone.	How dust free are the areas. Look under desks and behind work spaces to see if there is garbage and other unnecessary items.		
	XVI	Safety of the equipment, are areas gated off and safe for workers?	Spray shields and physical guards are in active use to keep items and liquids getting on the floor. Areas that are critical are clearly marked to protect workers.		
	XVII	Assess status of equipment in the area. Cleanliness overall appearance.	Are machines and equipment known to be on a schedule of cleaning?		
			Category Subtotal		
			Shine / Sweep Score: Subtotal divided by 5		
STANDARDIZE	XVIII	Is there visual color diagramming and color coding?	A clear and present color coding system is present in the work zone and across the company. It is clear that standards are being maintained and improved on.		
	XIX	Assess the access ways in case of emergency.	All emergency systems; fire vehicles, fire extinguishers, and emergency equipment free of obstruction and clear at all times. Access to electrical controls and fuses are known, marked, and free of any obstructions.		
	XX	The aisle ways are bright with light and clearly marked.	Walkways are clearly highlighted for direction, aisle access identified at any moment while in the work zone.		
	XXI	General area has quantity limits for materials and are marked clearly.	Heights are marked, quantity of materials are known, and min vs. max.		
	XXII	Is there clear document control of information in the work zone?	All information and documentation is controlled, labeled, and revisions are up to date. There are no label-less binders or pieces of paper in the area.		
			Category Subtotal		
			Standardize Score: Subtotal divided by 5		
SUSTAIN	XXIII	The aisle ways are clean and maintenance is clear.	Aisles are never full of anything and are clear for passage. All items and products not stored in the aisle and storage is next to aisle accessible for transportation.		
	XXIV	Illustrations and work zone plans are available to compare against.	5S has a maintenance system that allows for control of change and improvement of 5S in the work zones. Scoring is kept on each of these items and history is present and visible to support future improvement.		
	XXV	Ability for tools to be set back in place of storage.	No self-discipline is necessary to ensure that all tools, dies, jigs, and equipment are put back in the same spot. The effort of putting back should not require organizational skills.		
	XXVI	Evaluate the involvement of supervisors in 5S.	Supervisors are actively involved in the review process of 5S and are supporting improvement activities of the work areas.		
			Category Subtotal		
			Sustain Score: Subtotal divided by 4		

Total "Category Subtotals" divide by 26 average 5S score: TOTAL

5S Evaluation Review

Date: _____   Evaluation Area: _____

5S Element	Number	Evaluation Criteria	Rank these items from 1 through 5: 5 being well done	Score (1-5)	Ideas / Suggestions / Comments
SORT	I	Are the aisles and walkways open and clear?	All items that are not necessary or unsafe have been removed from the area where people travel and work.		
	II	Is the work zone free of any spills of fluids?	Consider whether there are any chemicals, lubricants, water, oils or other materials that may be hazardous in the area and on the floor.		
	III	Is the work zone free of unnecessary articles and items?	Are items that are not needed been removed from the work zone, i.e. tools, jigs, stationary, extra items.		
	IV	Is the work zone free of excess consumables/materials?	Evaluate against how many items are in the production work zone. Assess if the materials, parts, and supplies are currently needed for operations.		
	V	Is the information board active?	All announcements are displayed currently and in good presentable shape. Arrangement is straight and placed under appropriate headings.		
	VI	Are the areas walls and dividers free of items not used in operations?	Extra items are not on the walls, dividers, or hanging of signs that are not necessary.		
		Category Subtotal			
		Sort Score: Subtotal divided by 6			
SET IN ORDER / STRAIGHTEN	VII	Evaluate any documentation storage.	Only documents to do the job are stored at the work zone. These documents are stored nicely and in an orderly fashion that is recognizable to outsiders.		
	VIII	How are the shelves, desks, and work surfaces arranged?	All locations of items are labeled, marked, and it is known if they are missing.		
	IX	How are the tools and material used in operations stored?	No items are resting on walls or tucked in corners. No items are resting on equipment, cupboards, or other fixtures.		
	X	Evaluate container and packaging locations and tidiness.	Materials, boxes, storage containers, and other items are stored in the appropriate place and orientated well for operations. Also, they are secure and not causing any danger to the workforce.		
	XI	Assess order and where items are found on the floor.	Nothing is sitting directly on the floor and no materials are left around the area. Items that need to be on the floor are clearly marked and positioned in designated areas clearly outlined on the floor.		
	XII	Easiness to access the tools for machines and measuring gauges.	Materials, tools, jigs, attachments, and fixtures are organized so that they are all easily within reach of the operator. Consider this as well for any kind of measuring tool or go/no-go devices.		
		Category Subtotal			
		Set in Order / Straighten Score: Subtotal divided by 6			
SHINE / SWEEP	XIII	The storage of gauges and tooling.	Arrangement of all fixtures, tools, and attachments are kept in clean area for storage and no risk of damage during transporting to storage.		
	XIV	Clear when equipment needs maintenance and when last maintained.	Buttons and switches on machinery marked, highlighted, and labeled. Check sheets clean and displayed. Maintenance is scheduled; levels of fluids, lubrication of joints are clearly itemized and illustrated.		
	XV	Assess the cleanliness of the work zone.	How dust free are the areas. Look under desks and behind work spaces to see if there is garbage and other unnecessary items.		
	XVI	Safety of the equipment, are areas gated off and safe for workers?	Spray shields and physical guards are in active use to keep items and liquids getting on the floor. Areas that are critical are clearly marked to protect workers.		
	XVII	Assess status of equipment in the area. Cleanliness overall appearance.	Are machines and equipment known to be on a schedule of cleaning?		
		Category Subtotal			
		Shine / Sweep Score: Subtotal divided by 5			
STANDARDIZE	XVIII	Is there visual color diagramming and color coding?	A clear and present color coding system is present in the work zone and across the company. It is clear that standards are being maintained and improved on.		
	XIX	Assess the access ways in case of emergency.	All emergency systems; fire vehicles, fire extinguishers, and emergency equipment free of obstruction and clear at all times. Access to electrical controls and fuses are known, marked, and free of any obstructions.		
	XX	The aisle ways are bright with light and clearly marked.	Walkways are clearly highlighted for direction, aisle access identified at any moment while in the work zone.		
	XXI	General area has quantity limits for materials and are marked clearly.	Heights are marked, quantity of materials are known, and min vs. max.		
	XXII	Is there clear document control of information in the work zone?	All information and documentation is controlled, labeled, and revisions are up to date. There are no label-less binders or pieces of paper in the area.		
		Category Subtotal			
		Standardize Score: Subtotal divided by 5			
SUSTAIN	XXIII	The aisle ways are clean and maintenance is clear.	Aisles are never full of anything and are clear for passage. All items and products not stored in the aisle and storage is next to aisle accessible for transportation.		
	XXIV	Illustrations and work zone plans are available to compare against.	5S has a maintenance system that allows for control of change and improvement of 5S in the work zones. Scoring is kept on each of these items and history is present and visible to support future improvement.		
	XXV	Ability for tools to be set back in place of storage.	No self-discipline is necessary to ensure that all tools, dies, jigs, and equipment are put back in the same spot. The effort of putting back should not require organizational skills.		
	XXVI	Evaluate the involvement of supervisors in 5S.	Supervisors are actively involved in the review process of 5S and are supporting improvement activities of the work areas.		
		Category Subtotal			
		Sustain Score: Subtotal divided by 4		**Total "Category Subtotals" divide by 26 average 5S score: TOTAL**